Bobby Charlton's
Most Memorable
Matches

Bobby Charlton's Most Memorable Matches

Bobby Charlton

with Ken Jones

Cartoons by Roy Ullyett

Stanley Paul
London Melbourne Sydney Auckland Johannesburg

Stanley Paul & Co. Ltd

An imprint of the Hutchinson Publishing Group

17–21 Conway Street, London W1P 6JD

Hutchinson Publishing Group (Australia) Pty Ltd
PO Box 496, 16–22 Church Street, Hawthorne, Melbourne, Victoria 3122
PO Box 151, Broadway, New South Wales 2007

Hutchinson Group (NZ) Ltd
32–34 View Road, PO Box 40–086, Glenfield, Auckland 10

Hutchinson Group (SA) Pty Ltd
PO Box 337, Bergvlei 2012, South Africa

First published 1984
© Bobby Charlton 1984

Phototypeset by Input Typesetting Ltd, London SW19 8DR

Printed and bound in Great Britain by Anchor Brendon Ltd,
Tiptree, Essex

British Library Cataloguing in Publication Data

Charlton, Bobby
  Bobby Charlton's most memorable matches.
  1. Charlton, Bobby 2. Soccer players
  —Great Britain—Biography
  I. Title II. Jones, Ken
  796.33'4'0924   GV942.7.C48

ISBN 0 09 153580 8

Contents

Acknowledgements

I would like to thank Ken Jones whose work will be well known to readers of the *Sunday Mirror*. Ken is one of the few professional footballers to make a substantial career in sports journalism and his help and advice have been invaluable. Thanks also to Ken's daughter, Beverley, for her patience with the tape recorder.

Thanks are due to the following for allowing the use of copyright photographs: Colorsport, Central Press, Keystone Press, Press Association, Syndication International.

Introduction

When Sir Alf Ramsey invited me to join him during the long flight home from Mexico in June 1970, it was to apologize for not allowing me to complete what turned out to be my last game for England.

I'd been pulled off, controversially, in León where West Germany rallied to put us out of the World Cup in extra time, on the day that I overtook Billy Wright's record of 105 England caps.

It would be three months before Alf was again called upon to select an England squad and when he did my name was missing.

There was no announcement and quite frankly I would have been embarrassed by a ritual ending to my international career. Alf didn't go in for dramas so I fully understood when he didn't contact me.

People were left to draw their own conclusions and mine, at 33 years old, was that I'd worn England's colours for the last time.

Football offers no greater joy than that of playing so I continued to turn out for Manchester United and after that as Preston North End's player-manager.

But now it is about memories. Great players. Marvellous matches. The triumphs and the disappointments and a horrible day in Munich where so many of my friends perished.

Drawing from those memories, I have selected games that seem to stand out most in my mind: the World Cups of 1966 and 1970, the European Cup, the FA Cup and an army game played on an open field.

As the years roll by it is only natural for us to form retrospective judgements that suggest football isn't what it used to be.

Sir Matt Busby once said that the game was acquiring too much 'mind' and I believe this to be so. It lacks personalities, the distinctive, arousing touch of men like George Best, Denis Law, John Charles, Bobby Moore and Dave Mackay; it has become a different game for a different generation.

And yet for all football's problems – hooliganism on the terraces and the threat of bankruptcy in the boardrooms – it remains the best team game ever invented.

1 Western Command *v.* RAF

1956

He stopped and introduced himself one day in Wisbech, and though the face wasn't familiar, I certainly remembered the incident he began to describe. It happened during my army days. When in goal for an RAF team playing against Western Command, he was so startled by a ferocious shot from Duncan Edwards that he ducked and let the ball go into the net.

'That was the proudest moment of my life,' he chuckled.

The tale stayed with me and later, while driving across the flat Lincolnshire landscape, I began to dwell, not for the first time, on what Duncan might have achieved but for the horror of Munich.

What a footballer! What a man! Duncan looked indestructible, but no one is and fifteen days after being dragged from the wreckage at the end of the runway he was dead. Just twenty-one years old, he was already a legend.

Before I left home to join Manchester United, my uncles, who had been professionals, said, 'Be confident. Don't be frightened of anyone. Believe that you are the best.'

And I must admit that I fancied my chances. I'd scored twice for England Schoolboys at Wembley. All the big clubs had wanted to sign me. It had been said that I would play for England before I was twenty. I felt I was a good player. Then I saw Duncan Edwards.

I looked at him and thought, Bloody hell, who's this? At seventeen years old he was a man. A giant. And not only that, he could do everything I could do and more. He was fast and strong, two-footed, good in the air, and he read the game superbly. When Duncan swept forward with the ball at his feet you got the impression that it would take an antitank gun to stop him. Duncan didn't set out to make anyone feel inferior, but that's the effect he had upon me. I couldn't imagine ever being as good as he was.

Duncan didn't smoke or drink, and girls barely interested him. He lived for football, and by the time I turned up at Old Trafford he was already a first-team player. He was just sixteen when he made his debut, and on 2 April 1955, aged eighteen, he became the youngest player ever to appear in the full England side.

Sometimes when summer rain interrupts the coaching at my soccer schools, we sit around with the boys, talking about the game and I'm always thrilled if one of them, maybe just a ten-year-old, puts up a hand and says, 'Please, tell us about Duncan Edwards.'

Oh, I can tell them about Duncan. I can tell of his phenomenal ability, his enormous zest for football. His strength and courage. The power that brought him remarkable goals.

After we'd lost to Aston Villa in the 1957 FA Cup Final, so failing to win the Double, Matt Busby said, 'I have the finest young side in the world. All they need is experience to become the greatest, better even than Real Madrid. And in Duncan Edwards I believe I have the greatest footballer in the world. John Charles is bigger and has all the skills; Alfredo di Stefano is a mature artist. But Duncan Edwards is a footballer who can play anywhere without question and do a great job either scoring goals, preventing goals or knitting things together in midfield. The great thing about Duncan is that he always wants to be involved.'

Involved? You couldn't keep that big so-and-so out of anything and many's the time he simply brushed me aside in a practice match, going through as though I wasn't there.

What would he have achieved in the game? Well, when England won the World Cup in 1966, Duncan would have been thirty years old and, barring the injuries that began to be a problem quite early on in his tragically foreshortened career, at the peak of his powers. If Duncan's fitness had held up, I'm sure that he would have won a record number of England caps and, but for the accident, Manchester United would have dominated club football throughout the sixties.

I've heard it said that Bobby Moore benefited from Duncan's death, the popular assumption being that they played in the same position. Nonsense. Bobby was a master defender, marking space alongside the centre half; Duncan was much more of an all-purpose wing half, doing the job that Dave Mackay did so wonderfully well for Spurs. If he had lived Duncan would have controlled England's midfield using his tremendous strength and enormous energy to initiate and carry out attacks.

When the England manager Bobby Robson was still in charge at Ipswich, I remember him saying that, but for debilitating injuries, Kevin Beattie could have been the new Duncan Edwards. Don't believe it. Kevin was a fine player. Duncan was awesome.

Duncan was still eligible for the FA Youth Cup after he'd gained a regular place in the Manchester United first team and when he turned out for our youth team it didn't seem fair on the opposition.

I recall a two-legged semifinal against Chelsea, who were then beginning to get the best youngsters in the south as United had done in the north. More people showed up for those youth games than now go to watch First Division football at most grounds and there were over 20,000 to see us win 2–1 at Stamford Bridge. Chelsea were unlucky. They were the better team. The difference was that we had Duncan. He scored both our goals without any help. For one of them he ran forty yards, knocking a few people down on the way, before smashing the ball into the net. Then he was back defending the goal.

In the second leg at Old Trafford Duncan did it again. He had scored to make it 1–1, giving us a 3–2 aggregate lead, when I drove a corner kick to a point just outside the penalty area, opposite the far post. I'd seen him lurking there and knew that if the ball went within range he'd get to it. There were loads of players between Duncan and the goal, but he climbed above the lot and crashed the ball in with his head.

By then I was convinced that he was superhuman. It didn't matter if it was a kickabout in training or a match for England or United in the European Cup, Duncan always gave it everything. I think he was a little worried about getting too heavy because he trained like hell. One knee bothered him and he was prone to pulled muscles. But he was always pushing himself. Duncan would run and run.

When I progressed to the England Under-23 team, Duncan was established in the senior side and one day when both squads trained together, I was amazed by his confidence. Walter Winterbottom was the England manager and I imagine that when he selected the team Duncan's name was first on the sheet.

Professional players aren't overgenerous when it comes to praise. They aren't inclined to pat each other on the back. But that day Duncan was making well-established internationals catch their breath. He was moving onto balls, controlling them in a flash before sending them forty yards across field. He was arrogant but not in an objectionable way. It was just that he knew that he was a great player. There was no conceit in Duncan. But there were no question marks in his mind either. He didn't have to be told that he was the top man.

He was a smashing lad and I remember how glad I was to see him waiting by the barrack gates at Nescliffe, a Royal Army Ordnance Corps depot to which I was posted after completing my square bashing at Hilsea, near Portsmouth.

Those were the days of National Service and one result was that the British army for a number of years could put out a team that would now be worth millions of pounds. In my time we could have beaten anyone!

Our goalkeeper was Alan Hodgkinson of Sheffield United and England. The full backs were Alex Parker, then with Hearts and later with Everton and a Scottish international, and Graham Shaw of Sheffield United who was to play for England. Eddie Colman played; so did the great Dave Mackay. Cliff Jones, the Spurs and Wales flier, was on the left wing. Bill Curry of Newcastle, an outstanding goalscorer, was centre forward. We played, and beat, teams like Hearts, Tottenham and Rangers. We wiped out the army teams of Belgium and France.

The men in charge were Colonel Mitchell and Colonel Wilson. Colonel Wilson went on to become a general, but his great passion then was the army football team. Gerry Mitchell was a great guy too, for many years a prominent figure on the Football Association Council. Later on he loved to tell stories of how he helped us to develop as important footballers.

He had a particular affection for Jim Baxter, the great Rangers and Scotland halfback, who has been known to get into a few scrapes. It seems that Jim borrowed a fiver from Gerry one night when the army team, after my time, was touring in the Far East. Jim had long since been demobbed when he encountered Gerry again at some game or other.

'Colonel Mitchell, I owe you this,' said Jim, producing a five-pound note from his pocket.

Gerry was delighted. 'I always knew there was a lot of good in that lad,' he said.

Dear absent-minded Gerry, who once fell for one of Terry Venables's pranks.

'I'd like you to meet my brother,' said Terry. 'He's a terrific player and you're going to hear a lot of him.' Terry's 'brother' was Jimmy Tarbuck!

Anyway, the army got most of the young players during the National Service years and there's a story attached to how I got into the RAOC.

Nescliffe is between Oswestry and Shrewsbury, which was handy for Manchester, and when I was about to be called up the club told me to volunteer for the RAOC. Tradition is a big thing in the army so I had to tell a lie and say that my

father was in the RAOC. Dad was down the pit all his life but that didn't matter.

'Just tell them that he was in the RAOC and that you want to follow in his footsteps. With a bit of luck they'll fall for it and we'll get you posted nearby.'

It worked and off I went to Portsmouth for basic training. I didn't know what to expect and, filled with stories of how awful the food was, I treated myself to the best meal I could afford at Waterloo Station in London. As it happens, the food wasn't too bad, but that's more than I can say for the drill sergeant: I suppose that most of them are hard but this one was special. He terrified me and for weeks I saluted everyone in sight.

I was in the army when I played in the 1957 FA Cup final and the drill sergeant wrote me a letter:

'Dear Private Charlton, Hope that you've settled down in the army. I haven't seen you for a while but two friends would like to be at Wembley and I would be grateful for two tickets.'

He had to be joking!

I didn't like the army simply because it seemed to be interfering with my progress as a footballer, but like all old soldiers, I still think about the good times and particularly the friends I made. There was Del Hay, who was always saying, 'Give me fifty pounds and I'll be a millionaire in three years.' He wanted to have a market stall somewhere in the East End of London. 'Just £50. Just a start and I'll make it.' Perhaps he did, but I haven't seen him since the day I was demobbed.

And Roy Harms, who for years came to Manchester United matches in London. Having been born and brought up in the north, I suppose I thought that all Londoners were flash, but Roy had a terrific personality and we got on very well. Until we both got a forty-eight-hour pass I'd only seen Roy in uniform or denims and the transformation when he got dressed to go home was astonishing. A pin-striped suit and high white collar. He was immaculate. I still get a card from him at Christmas.

A lot of the lads promised to come and see me play after I was demobbed. Some did. Some didn't. Time goes by, and I suppose some of them thought that I wouldn't remember them. But Phil Stockel from Hartlepool used to come whenever we played in the northeast and I kept in touch with a few of the others for many years.

Strange days those army days. I'd look at my watch in the mornings and visualize what was going on at Old Trafford.

Ten o'clock. Tom Curry, the United trainer, would be coming out.

'Come on, hurry up. Stop messing about,' he'd be saying.

Eleven o'clock. Now they'd be doing some work on crosses. A bit of shooting practice perhaps.

Eleven thirty. Five-a-side.

Come midday, I'd feel better because training would almost be over and I wasn't missing anything.

If a plane passed overhead I'd imagine it was United off to some European game. It wasn't, of course, but that sort of thing goes through your mind. At least it went through mine.

Duncan Edwards had been demobbed by then, but for my first six months it was great to have him around.

He made a great fuss the day I arrived at Nescliffe. There he stood, huge as ever.

'Where have you been?' he inquired in that gruff voice of his. 'I thought you'd gone absent. Come on, we've got to get you settled in.'

The billet was the inevitable Nissen hut with a big black boiler in the middle. Duncan pointed to a bed that would be mine. Well, not quite because it wasn't sprung very well, so Duncan humped it out and came back with one that had belonged to somebody else. I don't know where he got it from, but it was a big improvement.

I didn't see much of Duncan because he always seemed to

be going away for matches, either for United or England, while I was still making my way in the game.

Not that he was getting rich. Like all professional footballers who were called upon for National Service, he was on a standard Football League contract of £7 per match and £5 per week in the close season. This was to protect the clubs in case their players were sent abroad. If you could get home to play you got paid. If you couldn't there was nothing, although payment of the statutory summer wage enabled the club to retain your registration.

But money didn't mean very much to us and I didn't give wages a second thought when I got the chance I'd been yearning for. Tommy Taylor, Dennis Viollet and Bill Whelan were down with injuries and so I was picked to play against Charlton. You can imagine what the headline writers made of that, particularly when I knocked in a couple of goals.

At the end of that season I played in the FA Cup Final against Aston Villa and when collecting my wages the following week I received the massive sum of £5 17s 6d in old money. Seven quid less tax! Duncan laughed about that.

I last saw him alive on the day I left hospital in Munich to return home by train. He was still battling for life, calling upon his immense reserves of strength to defeat the inevitable. Tears stained my face as I left that room, praying he would make it.

Back home in Ashington my mother would greet me each morning with the latest newspaper reports from the hospital. Sometimes the bulletins were optimistic and my hopes grew. Then one morning my mother said nothing. I knew there would be no more bulletins. Duncan was dead.

2 Manchester United *v.* West Bromwich Albion

FA Cup sixth round, 1958

As he gazed at a blank team sheet on 19 February 1958, with an FA Cup fifth-round tie against Sheffield Wednesday just a few hours away, Jimmy Murphy must have felt that he'd been entrusted with an impossible task.

Only thirteen days had elapsed since the horror of Munich. Many of Manchester United's finest footballers had perished; others had suffered wounds that would prevent them playing again; and it was feared that Matt Busby, who was still critically ill, might not recover sufficiently to resume his career at Old Trafford.

Jimmy escaped the accident by a curious twist of fate. Apart from being Matt's assistant, he managed Wales, who had been granted a totally unexpected chance to qualify for the World Cup to be staged in Sweden later that year, when an Arab country refused to play Israel and was disqualified. Israel were ordered to play one of the seven runners-up in the other groups and drew Wales, which is why Jimmy was on his way back from Cardiff instead of being in the seat next to Matt Busby, where our coach Bert Whalley died.

So to this tough but sentimental Welshman fell the enormous task of sustaining United through the blackest period in their history. Out of the sorrow and turmoil, blinking back tears that came frequently to his wise eyes, he cobbled together a team that went all the way to Wembley. It was a remarkable feat for which Jimmy deserved more credit than he got.

To meet immediate needs he signed Ernie Taylor, a crafty

little inside forward, from Blackpool and Stan Crowther from Aston Villa, a tough wing half whose tackles were the kind that linger on. Harry Gregg and Bill Foulkes survived the crash, more or less unscathed, and though I missed the match against Sheffield Wednesday, I rejoined the team shortly afterwards.

By then Wednesday had been swept aside and novices plucked from our third team were beginning to benefit from Jimmy's great skill and determination. I can hear him now, coaxing, pleading, occasionally cursing, filling us with his Welsh passion as each cup tie came around. It was said that we were carried to Wembley on a flood of emotion, but my impression was that Jimmy Murphy dragged us there.

Despite the number of opportunities – I believe Arsenal were among those keen to hire him – Jimmy never actually managed a Football League club, but there have been few better teachers of the game and I am greatly in his debt. Alf Ramsey helped me a lot when he became manager of England and so, of course, in many ways, did Matt Busby. But Jimmy got to my guts.

Greeting me at Exchange Station on the day I first reported to Manchester United, he was beamingly enthusiastic.

'Now then, Bobby,' he said, 'I've got a terrific footballer for you to play with. He's big, strong and quick. He can head. He can shoot. He can play the ball short or long. When I've smoothed the rough edges, this lad, Duncan Edwards, is going to be a great player.'

That was Jimmy. No nonsense. You could either play or you couldn't, and if you could, nothing was too much trouble.

There wasn't an apprenticeship scheme in those days and young players usually worked on the ground staff until they were old enough, at seventeen, to turn professional. This meant sweeping out the stands, cleaning boots, baths and toilets. My mother objected to that, so for two years I worked for an engineering company, training in the evenings, but most valuably on Sunday mornings when Jimmy gave me his undivided attention.

The fact that I'd played for England at Wembley as a schoolboy international was no guarantee that I would make the grade and I might not have but for Jimmy's dedicated tuition. He taught me what professional football is all about; it was a different game to the one I'd been playing.

I had the strength and timing to hit long passes across field, but I was made to appreciate that there was often more profit in playing the ball shorter, particularly if the long pass was likely to be cut out.

Jimmy would drag me out of practice matches to make a point, and I would stand there, half listening, one eye on the game, eager to get back into it. After a while I realized that I'd be kept there until Jimmy was satisfied that he was getting through.

Many years later, in punishing games for United and England, I had cause to be grateful for the hours spent under Jimmy's demanding scrutiny, the thousands of yards I chased for balls that he smashed from the centre circle to the four corners of Old Trafford so that I would learn that breathlessness wasn't an insurmountable barrier.

'Nobody has died of a heart attack on the pitch with me,' he'd shout, and off I'd go again, hunting another fifty-yarder!

I thought he was picking on me and one day I felt brave enough to say so.

'Why are you always on my back?' I asked angrily. 'Why don't you get on to the others?'

Jimmy pulled me to one side, draping a paternal arm around my shoulders.

'Listen, son,' he replied, the Rhondda Valley strong in his voice. 'We've got a lot of good young players here. Some of them will make it, some of them won't. We feel certain you will. That's why we give you so much of our time. Listen and learn.'

I didn't argue again.

Jimmy was responsible for the reserves, but his real joy was the youth team, who won the FA Youth Cup for the first five years of its existence. Even when we played on muck heaps, he made us feel that it was the most important game in which we were ever likely to be involved.

If we went out against a team in Birmingham, he'd say, 'We must win here because I can't stand Brummies.' In Yorkshire he couldn't stand Yorkshiremen. In the northeast he couldn't stand Geordies, and so on, until you began to suspect that he was the most prejudiced man alive. Then came a match in Cardiff.

'We've got to win here, boys,' he said, 'because I can't stand bloody Welshmen.'

We collapsed laughing.

Duncan Edwards was still playing for the youth team at that time and I remember one game down south, I think it was at Charlton, when he took a while to get going.

'When are we to see the genius then?' asked someone sarcastically from the opposition bench.

In that moment Duncan let fly from all of thirty yards and the ball flew into the net.

'That,' said Jimmy Murphy with a laugh, 'is Duncan Edwards.'

Apart from the small miracle he performed at Old Trafford in 1958, Jimmy did a fantastic job for Wales, taking them to the quarter finals of the World Cup, in which, when forced to play without the great John Charles, they narrowly lost to Brazil because the then seventeen-year-old Pele scored a freak in-off goal. Wales weren't thought to have any real chance in Sweden, but they responded marvellously to Jimmy's great powers of motivation and proved to be one of the big surprises.

Jimmy's team talks were always passionate and one delivered to the Welsh team before a match against England at Ninian Park, Cardiff, was a classic.

'See that lot across the corridor?' he said scornfully, a finger pointing in the general direction of England's dressing room. 'They come down here with little white shorts pulled up around their arses just to take the piss out of you, so let's get out there and give them something to remember us by.'

The Welsh tackling was characteristically ferocious, but Jimmy still wasn't satisfied when he confronted his men at half time.

'Come on, Jim,' protested one of the Welsh players. 'We're giving them some stick.'

'Giving them some stick, are we?' chided Jimmy. 'Well, you tell me why they keep getting up!'

On another occasion the Welsh players were sent out to face East Germany in a World Cup qualifying match with this information ringing in their ears.

'Now, don't forget, boys,' declared Jimmy as his team clattered out to do battle, 'this lot were shooting at your fathers a few years ago.'

Some people might find that offensive, but Jimmy didn't dislike the East Germans any more than he did the Brummies, the Geordies and the Cockneys who opposed Manchester United's youth team. He was just winding up his players.

In that respect he was from the old school, as were Bill Shankly, Bob Paisley, Joe Mercer and Stan Cullis, and I've always loved to hear tales about them and the people they knew. Great managers, they could impart more genuine wisdom with one imaginative phrase than you were likely to acquire on a hundred coaching courses.

Joe Mercer recalls a match in which Aston Villa were four goals down at half time, playing so miserably that he went to the dressing room in a great fury. When he got there, he found himself speechless. He gave the tea urn a mighty kick and walked out. Villa came alive in the second half, equalized and but for a missed penalty would have won.

One of Joe's best stories concerns the late Harry Storer, a great character and a formidable manager whose teams gave the impression that they were fed on iron filings. Joe was managing Sheffield United at the time and after a ferocious encounter with Derby County, where Storer was then in charge, he stated publicly that two of the Derby players should have been sent off. Storer, who wasn't at the match, telephoned Joe the following day and asked him to identify the offenders.

'Come on, Harry,' protested Joe, 'it wouldn't be fair on the two lads. I should hate to get them into trouble.'

'Get *them* into trouble,' retorted Storer. 'It's the other nine I want to sort out.'

No anthology of such tales would be complete without a substantial reference to Bill Shankly, who was, probably, the greatest character of them all. Whenever Liverpool played in Manchester they stayed at a hotel in Lymm, Cheshire, which was quite near to where I lived, and it wasn't unusual for Shanks to show up on my doorstep.

'Have you got a cup of tea?' he'd ask, and for an hour or so I'd be treated to a riot of comment on the game and life.

On one occasion he mentioned a youngster who had arrived at Anfield with a huge reputation. But Shanks wasn't all that impressed and when, after a month, he was asked how the lad was progressing, he muttered, 'Aye, he's got everything. Lice, VD . . .'

Many of Shanks's lines are firmly established in the folklore of the game, but his marvellous talent for imagery was so fertile that some of them have been mislaid in the harvest.

After signing Ron Yeats, the huge centre half who played such a prominent role in Liverpool's emergence as one of Europe's great teams, Shanks asked Everton's manager, Harry Catterick, if he'd seen the new man. Because of the great rivalry between Liverpool and Everton it was thought that Shanks and Harry never communicated, but this wasn't the case and Catterick admitted that he had yet to see Yeats play.

'Well, have a good look,' said Shanks. 'With this fella in the team we can afford to play Arthur Askey in goal!'

It was an immaculate image. Yeats was so dominant in the air that Liverpool were able to get the best out of Tommy Lawrence, a small but conspicuously alert goalkeeper who provided expert cover for a defence that was instructed to push up quickly behind the ball.

Apart from football, Shanks's other great passions were boxing and gangster movies. He loved the fight game – Jack Dempsey was one of his great heroes – and often used it, analogously, to impress a point upon his team; most colourfully, according to Emlyn Hughes, before an FA Cup semi-final replay against Leicester City at Villa Park, Birmingham.

Outplayed at Old Trafford, where Liverpool had missed chances, Leicester were given little hope in the replay, but Shanks was in no mood for complacency.

'We didn't see him until a few minutes before the kick-off,' recalls Emlyn. 'Then, suddenly, he was there, standing in that Jimmy Cagney pose, shoulders shrugging, hands thrust into the pockets of his raincoat.

' "How do you think they feel?" he asked, scanning the dressing room. "I'll tell you how they feel. They feel like someone who has gone in to fight George Foreman for the heavyweight championship of the world. Halfway through, the lights go out and he has to face Foreman all over again. That's how they feel. They've been battered and they've had three days to think about it. Now they are going to get battered all over again." It was brilliant stuff and the timing was perfect.'

Getting Shanks to concede a point wasn't easy, as his staff discovered on a tour of the United States. Liverpool had been in Chicago for a few days when Shanks joined them. Knowing how keen he was on boxing, Bob Paisley and Joe Fagan had arranged tickets for a local show, scheduled to begin a few hours after Shanks arrived.

'Boxing,' he growled. 'Christ, it's bloody midnight.'

When it was pointed out that there was a time-lag of five hours between Chicago and London, he turned away scornfully, growling, 'No bloody American is going to tell me what time of day it is.'

Bob Paisley eventually inherited the job to become the most successful manager in Europe and he too displayed a

distinctive style that maintained the flow of Anfield anecdotes. Bob's longer Geordie vowels are in soft contrast to the Scottish briskness of his predecessor but his lines can be just as cuttingly effective.

After galloping away with the First Division title yet again in the spring of 1983, Liverpool lost their competitive edge and completed the season with a string of uncharacteristic defeats.

'We got so bloody flash,' said Bob, 'that the skipper was tossing for ends with his American Express card.'

In telling these tales I could be accused of endorsing the view that managers and coaches are the most important people in the game. Some managers are inclined to encourage that belief and I find it irritating. The game is mostly about players. Alf Ramsey used to protest that managers get too much of the credit and too much of the blame, and I agree with him. There was a time when people wrote about football as they saw it; now most reporters seem obsessed with what the managers have got to say.

I remember vividly how it used to be when I first got into the Manchester United team. If you didn't play well, and that applied to everyone, you could expect to get hammered in the newspapers, and Henry Rose, a splendidly flamboyant figure who was among the eight writers who died in the Munich accident, could be scathing. He also awarded a weekly 'Rosette' and that was quite something for a young player to get.

Henry didn't survive to report the momentous events that led to the 1958 Cup Final when, to be fair, Jimmy Murphy was our principal strength. Jimmy persuaded me to sit next to him during the game against Sheffield Wednesday in that eerie fifth round, hoping, no doubt, that the atmosphere would rekindle my enthusiasm for football, so speeding my recovery from the crash. It was worse than playing against Norman Hunter or Tommy Smith! Jimmy kicked every ball, made every tackle and by the end of the game I was covered in bruises.

I came back quickly, and though our League form was feeble and uninspired, understandable when you consider that the team contained so many inexperienced players, we were a different team in the Cup. Drawn away to West Bromwich, where Jimmy had begun his professional career, we hung on to draw, so the scene was set for another unforgettable match at Old Trafford.

Jimmy was his usual galvanic self. An encouraging pat here. A reminder there. Come on, boys, this one we must win.

A hard match, it appeared to be heading for extra time when, after drifting to the right wing, I collected a pass and set off at the Albion defence. I couldn't hear Jimmy shouting from the bench but I expect he was. Get forward. Run them, Bobby. I got to the byline and cut the ball across, not aiming for anyone, simply hoping that someone would get a touch. Colin Webster did and we were through to the semifinals.

It always astonishes me when Johnny Haynes is omitted from lists of great postwar British footballers. He passed the ball brilliantly and had remarkable vision, so it was with some anxiety that we prepared to face Johnny's club, Fulham.

Another draw, 2–2 this time and lucky to get it. But what a different tale in the replay at Arsenal's ground, Highbury. Manchester United 5 – Fulham 3. The target had been reached.

I didn't expect us to beat Bolton in the final. They were a mature team who weren't about to be affected by the sentiment that had built up behind us. It was no great disappointment to lose at Wembley, not in the way that it had been the previous season. I hit a post with a shot that Eddie Hopkinson wouldn't have got to, but it was all over when Nat Lofthouse barged Harry Gregg, ball and all, into the net for Bolton's second goal.

I felt for Jimmy who, with Matt Busby well enough to attend the match but still frail sitting behind him on the touchline, was as committed as ever. He coaxed and he cursed, but we didn't have enough. I collected my losers' medal and headed slowly towards the dressing-room tunnel, a trip I was to make many times in the years up ahead. And I thought about another place and those who had perished there.

3 Leeds v. Manchester United

FA Cup semifinal replay, Nottingham, 1965

If Norman Hunter was on the other end of a tackle, few players were inclined to put a foot in; I certainly wasn't. A lovely lad, a tremendous defender who would have played more often for England if Bobby Moore hadn't been around, Norman was intimidatingly hard. It was said that if the wind was in the right direction when he came in from behind, you could hear that feared left foot cocking.

Those banners that proclaimed 'Norman Bites Yer Legs' weren't entirely an exaggeration, so when the ball fell between us during an FA Cup semifinal against Leeds United in 1965, my first instinct was to settle for being second best. Realizing how shameful that would be with 'Our Kid,' my brother Jack, playing for Leeds and my parents watching, I was tempted to be brave. Then I heard a familiar Geordie voice.

'Clatter the little bastard!' yelled Our Kid. I pulled out, deciding in an instant not to offer Norman the opportunity.

That was typical of Jack. He isn't as hard as he tries to make out, but being his brother didn't get me any privileges.

Leeds had been promoted the previous season after four years in the Second Division and their revival under Don Revie's astute management coincided with a change in Jack's fortunes. At thirty years old, an age when most footballers are beginning to wonder about what lies ahead, he suddenly came through as the outstanding centre half I'd always reckoned him to be and, fifteen months later, we fell into a tearful embrace on the Wembley turf after helping England to win the World Cup.

Revie, who built Leeds into one of Europe's most formidable teams, has been credited with transforming Jack's career, persuading him that there was no profit in the turbulence for which it had been conspicuous until then. During Revie's early days as manager at Elland Road there was a real threat that Leeds might sink into the Third Division. Jack, who had been dropped and put on the transfer list, was brought back into the team and the danger passed. Revie took him on one side and said, 'I want you to stay. If you keep going the way you are, there's no reason why you shouldn't play for England. You've got the ability, so it's only a matter of putting your mind to it.'

Maybe that sort of blunt approach was necessary, but I'm of the opinion that Jack simply responded to events that suggested he was no longer wasting his time at Leeds.

Independent, stubborn and rebellious, Our Kid loved the game but not the frustrating grind of simply playing for a living. He fell out with a succession of managers and coaches. Bill Shankly wanted him at Liverpool but jibbed at a fee of £18,500!

Things worked out well in the end. By the time Jack retired in 1972 to manage Middlesbrough, he was fully established as an international star.

Apart from a facial resemblance, we haven't much in common. He's older by two and a half years – he hates being reminded of that – taller and more physical.

Ken Jones wrote this about us in the *Sunday Mirror*:

The Charltons are so different in temperament, style, build and function, it is often difficult to accept that they are from the same set of parents.

They were born in Ashington, Northumberland, where the anonymous rows of colliers' cottages are either pointing towards the pit head or away from it. Sons of a miner, they were born into football. They are of the Milburns, a remarkable family whose prowess at the game has made them a legend in the northeast of England.

At one time there were four Milburns, Jack, George, Jimmy and Stan, playing at fullback in the Football League. They were not graceful or articulate players. They were hard, uncompromising, their style reflecting the harshness of the environment in which they were raised. Miners are not likely to worry overmuch about a kick on the shin when they live with the prospect of the roof coming in.

There is much of the Charltons' uncles in the play of Jack. A lot of Jackie Milburn, their mother's cousin, in Bobby's style.

Devastatingly quick and armed with a murderous shot, Jackie helped to bring three FA Cups back to Tyneside and assured himself of immortal recall in the history of Newcastle United.

You never get the impression that the Charltons are close like some brothers are close. It is almost a casual relationship and their approach to life couldn't be more different. Bobby's affairs are well ordered. Jack is of the outdoors. A hunter, a fisherman. He likes the wind in his face and is never more contented than with a gun or a rod in his hand.

That is a fair summing-up. If Jack's around Manchester he might call in for a chat and a cup of tea, and we meet at matches and dinners, but we don't live in each other's pockets.

Like most elder brothers, Jack regarded me as a pest when we were kids, especially when I'd plead to go with him to pick potatoes or on fishing trips to the river at Bothal, a tiny village close to where we lived.

'He's not coming,' Jack would say defiantly.

'You take him,' my mother would insist. From then on it would be nothing but moans and there are people who will suggest that he's never stopped moaning.

Jack was beginning to make a name for himself in local football and one day he turned out in a cup tie at Hurst Welfare. That was the big time. An enclosed pitch, nets and a crowd clustered enthusiastically around the touchlines. I was playing nearby – no nets for us – and after we'd heard a great shout, someone reported that Jack had given away a penalty.

By the time he got home I was perched on a chair in the living room.

'Fancy giving away a penalty,' I said cheekily. Not bothering to break stride, Jack hit me a smack on the head and I fell to the floor, yelling. Jack got thumped for that, but it wasn't about to change him. He's never tried to conceal his darker moods and once his mind is made up nothing will alter it.

We began to go our separate ways when Jack signed for Leeds, though when I eventually got to Old Trafford I often went over the Pennines to watch him play. I'd made the first team by then and it used to bother me that things didn't seem to be going as well for Our Kid. I was with a glamorous club who were chasing the big prizes whereas Leeds seemed to be struggling. If he'd sensed my sympathy I might have got another crack on the head, but that was long ago. Since then, of course, things have gone marvellously well for him.

When I'd recovered sufficiently to travel home by train from Munich following the accident, Jack met me in London and drove me to Ashington where I was to spend a week or two. He didn't say much and there were long silences during the journey. But I felt very close to him then.

Leeds weren't the most popular team in the land, achieving a level of professionalism that many people found unacceptable. They didn't miss a thing and one or two of their players had a reputation for 'going over the top', a mean, potentially damaging trick that sends the tackling foot in above the ball.

Jack was never guilty of that. He was tough, of course, but never dirty. Much fuss was made over his claim to have a little black book that was supposed to contain the names of players upon whom revenge was to be taken. I didn't believe it, though I'm sure Jack made mental notes.

One of Leeds's ploys involved sending Jack forward to stand in front of the opposing goalkeeper at corner kicks. When he did so he'd come in for some stick from the crowd. They were wasting their breath.

Our Kid turned out to be a marvellous player for England,

and Gordon Banks had a lot to thank him for. A great goal-keeper in every other respect, Gordon didn't always get cleanly to crosses. So Alf Ramsey made Jack responsible for attacking the ball when it came high into the penalty area at corners and free kicks. Few people noticed, but Jack didn't mark anyone in those circumstances. He simply went for the ball with his head.

Jack came into the England team after Maurice Norman of Spurs broke a leg, but not before Alf had put him through a serious test at Hampden Park, Glasgow. Chosen to play for the Football League against the Scottish League, he found himself marking John Hughes of Celtic, a burly but skilful centre forward who continually lured Jack out of position.

In the first half he was guilty of following Hughes into midfield, leaving gaps that the Scots were quick to exploit. Alf said nothing to Jack at half time. The answer was to shunt Hughes onto the midfield and Jack came up with it. Alf had found himself a centre half.

By then Jack was already a fully qualified coach and later on, when managing Middlesbrough and Sheffield Wednesday, he was able to apply his tactical know-how.

Mind you, any club that employs Jack must accept his refusal to be concerned with anything he regards as irrelevant detail. He has been known to forget the names of his own players. A friend who rang to ask where Sheffield Wednesday would be staying prior to a match in London, was told, 'No idea. I just get on the bus.'

Two of the Sheffield Wednesday players weren't on the bus when it arrived at Highbury for an FA Cup semifinal against Brighton in 1983. Jack had left without them. Far from being embarrassed, while waiting for them to turn up in a taxi, Jack told the story to a television commentator who immediately repeated it to the nation.

'For goodness sake,' protested Jack's chairman. 'Why didn't you keep it quiet?'

'I thought it was a good story,' replied Jack.

35

Neil Phillips, doctor to the England team during the 1970 World Cup in Mexico and still a good friend to both of us, was behind Jack's appointment at Middlesbrough. Having made the initial approach by telephone, Neil, who was then vice-chairman, made an appointment to meet Jack.

'You name the place,' said Neil.

Jack nominated a hotel that was situated, conveniently, halfway between Leeds and Middlesbrough. Neil arrived to discover that the hotel had been demolished!

Neil was in the dressing room at Ayresome Park when, some forty-five minutes before a match, one of the players collapsed with severe stomach pains. Grabbing the telephone, he called Jack who was in his office.

'What do you want me to do about it?' said Jack. 'You're the bloody doctor.'

But some quick thinking was going on. Jack unearthed one of his reserves from the crowd and put him into the team instead of another lad who was already half stripped. He also included the substitute in the team and Middlesbrough beat Ipswich 2–1!

A house guest once asked to see Jack's medals. After a long search they were discovered in a cigar box, mixed up with buttons and safetypins.

But don't be misled. A shrewd lad is Our Kid. He's done well, not only in football but on television with programmes that highlight his passion for fishing and field sports. He's got a lovely house in Yorkshire and a charming little villa in Spain. He speaks brilliantly at numerous dinners.

He shoots with the royal family and is on first-name terms with quite a few of them. What else, because Jack is never likely to bow and scrape. His motto is: 'Take me as I am or not at all.'

He was a Guardsman in the army and when we were about to be presented to the Queen before the World Cup final he said, 'I'm going to ask her if she remembers me walking up and down outside her window.'

Thinking better of it, he settled for a bow and handshake.

We played against each other quite often after Leeds returned to the First Division, but the semifinal at Hillsbrough, Sheffield, attracted most attention because it was unusual for brothers to be competing for a place at Wembley.

How did I feel? How did he feel? What did the family think? The questions were endless, and Jack telephoned me to say that he wasn't going to get involved with the newspapers who were pressing for special articles.

After a goalless draw, we met again in the replay at Nottingham the following Wednesday.

I didn't enjoy playing against Leeds. There was no humour in their football and, as Matt Busby used to say of the game when it began to become more organized, there was 'too much mind'. Leeds could play marvellously but they always seemed to be on a tight rein. I never got the impression that they were enjoying themselves. They were sour, winning was all, and they were paranoid about criticism. They beat us that night, little Billy Bremner sneaking in to get the only goal.

It's rotten when you lose in a semifinal. All that effort and nothing to show. I was sitting slumped in the dressing room when Our Kid came beaming through the door.

Go away, I thought. We don't need you at this moment.

But Jack just stood there, the smile getting wider and wider. 'Hey,' he said, 'I've been picked for England.'

The news had been kept from him until after that match – typical Leeds – and now he had to tell me!

'That's terrific,' I said.

I just wish he'd told me some other time.

4 Benfica v.
Manchester United

European Cup, 1966

For an all too brief spell George Best was probably the world's supreme footballer. He could shoot, dribble, pass, head and tackle. He was murderously quick; he was brave, strong, imaginative and astonishingly cool. What more could you ask? Well, you could have asked him to turn up now and again.

George became about as reliable as a rusty watch. If he showed up on time, it was an event. Sometimes he didn't show up at all. By then he seemed to be appearing in the gossip columns more frequently than on the sports pages, and a succession of stunningly attractive females was decorating his life.

It has been said that George was as symbolic of his age as the Beatles were. There is no doubt that his extravagant style, both on and off the field, appealed instantly to a generation that mutinied against traditional values and ideals. But time waits for no athlete and it wasn't about to slow respectfully to a crawl for the high-flying Ulsterman; within five seasons of being voted European Footballer of the Year in 1968, George had come to the end of his first-class career. He was just twenty-six years old.

The demons had caught up and George eventually admitted to being an alcoholic, his mind a confusion of broken promises and blighted dreams. He could and should have been the greatest player of all times, better even than Pele and di Stefano, and in failing to achieve that pinnacle, to establish himself fully as one of the game's great heroes, I believe he contributed vastly to the decline of British football.

For a while everything about George was heroic: a working-class upbringing in the raw, red-bricked streets of Belfast; the inventive application of immaculate skill; courage; dark good looks. If only he had lasted longer. He might have done but for the savage physical and emotional blows Matt Busby took at Munich that awful day in February 1958. After losing a team, people that he loved and almost his own life, Matt became understandably more pragmatic, and George, who signed for United as an amateur in 1961, was never really exposed to the discipline I experienced during my early days at Old Trafford. I could see the sense in allowing George to develop naturally, but once the wayward aspect of his nature began to surface, Matt should have been unyieldingly firm. 'The rest will come in time,' he said when ordering his staff not to tamper with George's progress.

It certainly did; not only memorable feats of skill and daring that added greatly to Manchester United's stature as one of the world's great football clubs, but the scandal, the bitter recriminations and ultimately, of course, a tragically premature extinction.

George was so painfully shy when he first stepped off the boat from Belfast that Matt may have been fooled into believing he would be no more difficult to handle than any of us had been, particularly Duncan Edwards, the greatest of his 'Babes'. A boy among men, a man among boys, Duncan took stardom in his powerful stride and remained marvellously unspoiled, though to be fair, circumstances had changed dramatically when George came upon the scene.

There was no longer a ceiling on salaries. Prior to 1961 the maximum weekly wage laid down by the Football League was a derisory £20 during the playing months and £17 in the close season, and the 'retain and transfer' system that bonded a player for life to whichever club held his registration was about to be ruled illegal. Greater earning power gave professional footballers a new status and for a young man with

George's immense gifts the horizons must have appeared unlimited.

We had little in common beyond the colours of Manchester United. Seven years George's senior, I had settled down to married life when he began to assume the image of a pop star, responding instantly to the mood that was gathering momentum throughout the land. It was all there: the Beatle haircut, the trendy gear, the white Jaguar saloon, the braceleted entourage of hangers-on who persuaded him that conformity was for kicking into touch.

Sometimes during a pause in training, a stroll between sprints, I would inquire mischievously about the previous night's activities. 'How was it at the Black Cat?' I'd ask, inventing the name of a night club.

Giving me an indulgent smile, wanting no part of such nonsense, George would surge away into the distance.

A good marriage might have worked for George, and once, in strange circumstances, I got the impression that he was keen to settle down. We'd played for the Rest of the United Kingdom against Wales at Cardiff and next day, on the journey back, I invited George home. Never having much to say to each other, we'd hardly spoken since leaving Wales, so I was astonished when George agreed to get off the train at Crewe where, for convenience, I'd left my car. My wife and daughters were away and George settled on a settee in the lounge, feet up, watching TV, flicking through magazines while I fixed a meal. When we'd eaten he sat back and began to ask questions that were entirely out of character.

'Who does your garden, Bob?'

I told him that a man came in once a week to keep it tidy.

He asked if Norma had anyone to clean. He wanted to know how much the carpets and the furniture cost.

I was baffled. Then it came to me. George was thinking about getting married.

'That's it,' I said to Norma when she returned the following day. 'That's why he came here. He wanted to see what family life was like.'

Sure enough, within a few weeks, George had established a serious relationship with Eva Haraldsted, a pretty Danish girl he'd met on tour, and she came to join him in Manchester. But the 'engagement' didn't last and it wasn't long before he bought a ludicrously gadgeted house in Bramhall where, besieged by curious sightseers, he often sat brooding with only the demons for company.

He was obsessed with the idea that he wouldn't live past his thirty-fifth year and, pursued by the dark vision of mortality that afflicts most of us, he became even more unreliable. Hounded by the press and television, which must accept some of the blame for his destruction, George blundered from one outrageous escapade to another.

Rather than suffer the aggravation of refusing requests for appointments, George granted them all but with little or no intention of turning up. On one occasion he failed to keep a lunch date with Michael Parkinson and the film actor Rod Steiger in London. When, after two hours, it was clear that George wasn't going to appear, Mike apologized to his famous companion.

Steiger smiled. 'That's how it is with superstars,' he said philosophically.

George's agent at that time was Ken-Stanley, a former England table tennis international who also handled Denis Law. I hope Ken did well out of the deal because it was a thankless task. I recall Ken turning up at the Cliff, United's training ground in Salford, with the latest product to bear George's name, chewing gum, the wrapper of which featured him performing various football skills. Without bothering to examine the design, George popped the gum into his mouth and threw the wrapper away. He was by then at the mercy of uncontrollable impulses.

Boxing experts have told me that great fighters can come apart without warning, discovering suddenly, in one bout too many, that the messages are no longer travelling as swiftly from the brain. The process of decline is more gradual in a footballer but, as he approaches the end of his career, there are usually telltale signs.

For instance, I remember playing against Spurs at Old Trafford when we were told to take the ball past Danny Blanchflower, their great Irish international captain. Danny's artistry, wisdom and generalship had been central to Tottenham's great triumphs in the early sixties, but time and injury had so reduced his scope and mobility, he was there to be taken. The party was over for him that day.

In George Best's case the brilliant flame began to flicker and dim when he lost the blinding speed which, when allied to exceptional change of pace, was the most crucial element in his game.

George Cohen, the former Fulham and England fullback who was perhaps the most underestimated member of the 1966 World Cup winning team, says, 'Apart from being astonishingly skilful, George was very quick off the mark, which made him a handful in the penalty area. I don't think I came across anyone who managed to get so many steps into a short distance. I wasn't slow and I knew enough about the game to shunt wingers into places where they were no longer dangerous. I could even do that with Bestie when he was used out on the touchline and I remember Jimmy Langley, who was our other fullback at the time, having a particularly good game against him. But once George was given licence to use the full width of the pitch, you could look out. In the mood, he could beat you down either side and usually did.

'In those days he had a tremendous appetite for the game and was always prepared to tackle back if he lost the ball. Manchester United's forwards were never keen on doing that, so if you robbed one of them there was usually an opportunity to go at their defence.

'But if George lost the ball he was almost desperate to get it back and he was there, snapping at your heels.'

That testimony emphasizes the commitment George Best had to the game until erosion set in. I'm convinced that he set out to be the greatest player on earth, a status he might well have achieved but for that crazy lifestyle.

George wasn't easy to play with and there was no point trying to involve him in schemes that required the cooperation of other players like Denis Law, who for all his great prowess as a goalscorer was marvellously astute if he sensed an opportunity to put someone else in for a strike at goal.

'Look for Denis, knock the ball in to him and go for the return,' Jimmy Murphy used to say. 'That way you'll score twice as many goals.'

George would nod his head and carry on his own sweet way as he once did, much to the frustration of his Irish teammates, in a match against Russia in Belfast. The Russians had set a disciplined marker on George and no matter what he tried he couldn't get free. The obvious solution was to play a one–two. Most players would have settled for that. But not George. The more difficult things became the more intent he was on showing who was boss. He didn't succeed.

We used to say that George would never take up golf because he hated parting with the ball and that the most unselfish run in football was one in support of him.

I was far from being the perfect team player and a tendency to select the wrong option – long passes when shorter ones were more profitable and certainly safer – remained a flaw throughout my career. But George carried individualism to an extreme and, however exciting this may have been for the onlooker, it was maddening when the team suffered.

That experience became so commonplace that I decided to wait for an opportunity to ignore him. It came in a match against Nottingham Forest when we were two goals ahead with only a few minutes left. George was out on the left touchline, poised as he so often was, head up, the ball under perfect control, frustrating the tackles that were being launched at him.

Right, I thought, this time you aren't getting any help, and I stood still.

George came infield and passed me at a gallop, heading

for the opposite touchline, the fullback in close pursuit. I still hadn't moved. What would George do now? Back he came, from right to left, and once again I watched him go by. He was back where he started. I was still stationary when George decided to cross my path again, but it had got beyond a joke.

'You greedy little . . . What a bloody goal!' Before I could complete the curse, George had crashed the ball into the roof of the net. What could you do with him?

In five full seasons between 1966 and 1971, George scored ninety league goals for Manchester United, an impressive striking rate that was augmented in the various cup competitions and when wearing the green of Northern Ireland.

Many of his goals were classics of improvisation and I particularly remember one he got against Real Madrid in the European Cup semifinals, a goal that was to prove invaluable when we travelled to Spain for a momentous second leg.

John Aston had set off down the left wing and, anticipating the centre, George began to move in from the opposite flank shadowed, of course, by a defender. Then came that bewildering change of pace as he surged clear, gaining a yard or two of room. He was running at right angles to the goal and I'm sure that he intended to strike the ball clean with his left foot, which made the subsequent execution all the more remarkable. At the very last second, the ball bobbled, a bad bounce that would have caused most players to miscue. Not George. Making the merest adjustment at top speed, he half-volleyed a ferocious scoring shot.

In his book, *There's Only One United* (1978), my dear friend Geoffrey Green, for many years the most distinguished of football writers, describes that moment like this: 'It might have been Walter Hammond driving a half volley gloriously past extra cover off the full meat of the bat. Old Trafford exploded, a frightened cat ran the full length of the pitch, and one felt that here at last, in another sense, the cat had really been set amongst the Spanish pigeons.'

It was in another European Cup tie, a quarter final against

Benfica in 1965, that George played, what I believe to be, his finest game.

The previous year, at the same stage of the Cup Winners' Cup, we'd squandered a 4–1 home lead against Sporting Lisbon by collapsing 0–5 in the Portuguese capital. Harsh words were spoken in our dressing room that night and Matt Busby's humour didn't improve when it was suggested in the newspapers back home that a less arrogant club would have adopted more sensible tactics. With a three-goal cushion, we probably were complacent, but football is mostly about players and Matt could not have budgeted for our pathetic form.

That defeat lived with us for a long while, so when we were drawn to play Benfica in March 1966 I tingled with anticipation. Here was a chance to redeem ourselves.

Benfica had become a great power in the game and a few months later I was to face six of their stars, including Eusebio, when playing for England against Portugal in the World Cup semifinals at Wembley. They'd twice won the European Cup. They'd reached the final four times in five years, and it was seven years since they had lost at home in any European competition.

A huge eagle stands above the Estadio da Luz – Stadium of Light – and to play beneath its perch, in the presence of 75,000 people, was indeed an experience.

After winning narrowly, 3–2, at Old Trafford, we travelled to Lisbon aware that there was a tough night ahead. As our bus nosed through the crowds, Benfica supporters beat upon the windows and, remembering how their great rivals had humiliated us a year earlier, they mocked us with their fingers indicating another 0–5 defeat. We were hardened to that sort of experience and I remember saying to Shay Brennan, who sat next to me, 'Won't it be marvellous if the score is the other way round.'

Our instructions were to play it tight for twenty minutes. We were kept waiting that long while Eusebio was presented with his European Footballer of the Year trophy. George was to say later that Matt's twenty minutes were used up in the dressing room! We fidgeted, as most footballers do before the kick-off, going through all the familiar little rituals, and it was then that Pat Crerand broke a mirror. The dressing room went silent.

'For Christ's sake, Paddy,' someone said. 'That's all we effing well need.'

Forty-five minutes later, when we clattered back into the dressing room leading 3–0 – 6–2 ahead on aggregate – Paddy called out, 'Anyone got another mirror?'

A year earlier Matt had confronted us angrily in Lisbon. Now there was a satisfied beam on his face and no wonder. We really had set out to contain Benfica for a while, but within fifteen minutes of the kick-off they'd been torn to pieces by George Best's genius.

In Germano, Cavem, Cruz, Pinto and Coluna, the Portuguese had a wealth of defensive experience, so it was astonishing that they should allow George opportunities to get behind them. We'd been playing for only a few minutes when I was pulled down. Tony Dunne took the free kick and George darted across two men, timing his jump perfectly to head past Costa Pereira. The vast crowd was stunned and when I glanced upwards even the eagle looked sick!

That was only the beginning. Selecting the safe option, I slid the ball back to Harry Gregg and he thumped it upfield. David Herd got a touch with his head and there was George, threading his way past three opponents, leaving them all for dead with his blinding speed. Two – nil! I thought the eagle was going to tumble from its perch.

When John Connelly got our third, swooping onto Denis Law's pass, we knew it was all over.

Eusebio, the great hero of Benfica, whose hat trick had destroyed Real Madrid in the European Cup final three years earlier, tried desperately to bring his team back from the dead. His free kicks were struck so wickedly and with such venom that I couldn't help feeling how difficult the game would have been had we not taken it over so quickly. But even when Shay Brennan unluckily put the ball into his own goal, I had no doubts that we would win. George continued to be fantastic, changing direction so bewilderingly and at such speed that Benfica didn't know what to do with him. A fourth goal came when Denis Law put Pat Crerand in and I got the fifth a few minutes from time.

'This,' declared a jubilant Matt Busby afterwards, 'is one of the great moments in my life.'

We had triumphed in the most testing of circumstances and in a way that fully represented Matt's ideals.

But it had been George's night and, despite their great disappointment, the Portuguese warmed to his artistry. They christened him 'El Beatle'. He was now an international star. Europe was raving about him.

Had we won the European Cup that season instead of going out to Partisan of Belgrade in the semifinals, George might have avoided some of the traps into which he fell. His ego would have been satisfied for a while, making it easier to live with the knowledge that there was no place for him in the World Cup, the greatest of football's stages. George was willing to work for the international stardom he craved; it was only when frustration set in that he began to neglect his training.

I often wonder whether things would have worked out differently for George had he been able to play for England or, indeed, Scotland. I'm sure that he was proud to play for Northern Ireland but, with respect, Windsor Park, Belfast, isn't quite the same as Wembley or Hampden Park. There were no World Cups for George and for a player with his enormous talent that was a tragedy.

The division of nationalities in Great Britain baffles people abroad, particularly in South America where they cannot understand why we should want to send out four teams or, indeed, why we should be allowed that distinction.

Sidling up to one of my mates during the 1970 World Cup, a Mexican journalist claimed, in a whisper, to be in possession

of a secret that would provide absolute proof of Alf Ramsey's fallibility.

'Tell me why Ramsey does not pick George Best?' asked the Mexican. 'Anyone who ignores such a player as this must be a fool.'

'Ramsey cannot pick Best,' said my pal. 'George can only play for Northern Ireland.'

'Ah,' said the Mexican, gleefully preparing to disclose the information he had uncovered. 'I have seen George Best's passport. I have also seen that of Bobby Moore. They are the same.'

As the late Eric Morecambe might have said, there is no answer to that.

Those who remain paranoid about Alf and his strategy might argue that because George was essentially a winger he wouldn't have got a game for England anyway. But Alf wasn't opposed to wingers, only to the idea that they should be left out wide, waiting for the ball. Alf might not have used George as a winger, but he would have been in the team.

'A magnificent footballer,' said Alf one night. And, of course, George was.

I wasn't surprised when he didn't turn out for my testimonial game in September 1972. We were never close friends, and by then I sensed a definite sourness, a clear resentment of the bond I had with the club. He also knew that I felt he'd taken far too many liberties.

In his revealing autobiography, *Where Do I Go from Here?*, George states that he wasn't the only Manchester United player to believe that I should have retired much earlier than I did, but that the others were reluctant to speak up in public as he did. Looking back, recalling remarks that were passed from time to time, I'm sure that's true.

I bear George no grudges. It was a privilege to play with him and to marvel at his skills.

5   England *v*. Finland, Norway, Denmark and Poland

Pre-World Cup tour, 1966

A glance at the team sheet told me that I had been selected to wash up on Wednesday. What, you may well ask, did that have to do with England winning the 1966 World Cup? Well, it was like this. Alf Ramsey – he was still plain Alf then – had decided that we would begin our preparation at Lilleshall in Shropshire, a stately home that had been given to the British government some years previously for use as a National Recreation Centre.

Carriages may have once brought the local gentry to Lilleshall's noble doors, and when there was time to relax in the lovely old high-ceilinged rooms I could imagine the finery of grand gatherings. But for us, the England footballers from whom Alf would choose twenty-two for the World Cup squad, there was to be no gracious living. It wasn't quite like being back in the army, but almost!

We slept in dormitories, stood in line for our meals and took turns at doing the dishes. We queued to make telephone calls from a coin box at the foot of an elegant period staircase and there were no week-end passes. As for nights out – well, we got one during the entire fortnight, when Alf *ordered* us to join him for a beer at the local golf club.

Lilleshall was, and still is, the main centre for Football Association coaching courses and I'd heard some lurid tales from lads who'd been there. One or two pubs in the area were famous throughout the game, but Alf made it abundantly clear that any of us who wanted to sample them could forget about playing in the World Cup.

As a coaching centre Lilleshall had become synonymous with fancy phrases and theories that irritated some of the older professionals. One of them told me that he had been asked on a course to state why British footballers lacked 'environmental awareness'. Sarcastically, he replied, 'Because we didn't get enough meat during the war.'

But Lilleshall was where we did the basic work that was to prove invaluable during the weeks that lay ahead. I loved it. Football was my life and I was with footballers, playing football. We were all in good shape after a full League season, but that wasn't good enough for Alf and his trainers, Harold Shepherdson and Les Cocker. Time would tell whether there was a better team, but no team would be fitter.

The work was so strenuous that when the press lads were allowed in for a day they were convinced that a punishing session had been put on especially to impress them. That was definitely not the case. Most nights we were looking for our beds long before lights out. Sometimes I lay there reflecting on what had struck me in Chile four years earlier – that we were more than capable of winning the World Cup when it was staged in our homeland. The host nation invariably did well and by 1966 some of us should have fully matured as international footballers. Nor had I seen anything in Chile to suggest that any truly great teams might be in the making. And Alf Ramsey hadn't entered into my calculations that summer in South America, but he did now!

When Alf succeeded Walter Winterbottom as England manager in 1963, I didn't know what to expect. He'd been a stylish fullback and made a great impression as manager of Ipswich, bringing them forward from the Third Division to win the League championship, employing tactics that had bemused our best teams. So were we about to be committed to a style that would suppress initiative and flair? It may come as a surprise to Alf's critics, but that was never the case. To my knowledge, Alf never told anyone how to play for England. He had a system and chose people who could make that system work simply by doing the jobs they did for their clubs. By establishing a mobile bulwark in midfield, Alf more than anyone influenced the way football is now played, but he cannot be held responsible for the follies of his imitators.

A truly great manager, Alf believed above all in individual ability. He would curse you if the ball was given away carelessly. 'Think of the ball as a jewel,' he would say. 'Covet it, caress it.' He impressed on us that we should be well organized against free kicks and corners. If a goal was given away in such situations, he regarded it as a crime. He deplored poor finishing. But to new players coming into the team he only ever said two things: 'Just do what you are used to doing. Good luck.' He could be caustic, he remains sensitive, he was always immensely loyal and occasionally very funny in a dry way.

As a senior member of the squad I was once asked by the other players to approach Alf for permission to travel in casual gear rather than in the outrageously heavy suits that had been provided by the Football Association. 'I'm always open to suggestions,' said Alf. 'Yes, we'll travel in the suits.'

Once, when arriving in Glasgow, we were met at the airport by a posse of Scottish reporters. One of them, a dapper little man, stepped forward and offered Alf his hand. 'Welcome back to Scotland,' he said.

'You must be joking,' replied Alf. He never did get on with the Jocks.

One summer in Canada a brash, red-blazered radio interviewer almost speared Alf with a microphone. 'Sir Alf,' he declared, 'we're giving you ten minutes of CBC time.'

Alf swerved past him without breaking stride. 'Oh, no, you're not,' he said, tossing the phrase back over his shoulder.

Geoff Hurst recalls giving Alf a lift from Heathrow Airport after a match in Northern Ireland. When they pulled up outside the Football Association offices at Lancaster Gate in London, Geoff reached across to open the passenger door, saying, 'There you are, Alf. See you at the next game.'

'Yes, Geoff,' replied Alf, 'I'll see that you get a couple of tickets.'

The day after we'd won the World Cup, Alf was approached by three sportswriters who knew him well. 'Can you spare ten minutes?' they asked.

Alf kept on walking. 'It's my day off,' he replied and meant it.

Alf Ramsey wasn't exactly a sportswriter's dream and his attitude to the press and television contrasted sharply with that of Sir Matt Busby, who was a master of public relations. But they certainly had one thing in common. Liberties were not allowed.

Players will try it on with a new manager, testing the ground, seeing how far they can go. Alf made no allowances.

We were in Lisbon to play Portugal and at curfew time there were a few empty beds. Alf wasn't waiting to make a huge fuss when we came in an hour late. But can you imagine the panic when word got around that he was sending us home in disgrace. There would be cameramen and reporters at the airport, embarrassing headlines to account for. We didn't get much sleep that night.

The following morning Alf did nothing until he had finished his breakfast. Then he said, 'There are people here who need to see me.' The admonishment, delivered in private, was severe. 'If replacements had been available you would now all be on a plane back to England,' said Alf. No one ever broke curfew again.

No one did at Lilleshall that summer of 1966, though a few got their knuckles rapped one night for wandering out of bounds. The days drew on and you could sense a slight tremor of nervousness about the place. As an established member of the England team I didn't have to concern myself with the possibility that I might not play in the World Cup. But that didn't apply to everyone and before we left for a summer tour Alf would have to jettison four or five players.

Peter Thompson of Liverpool, a hugely talented forward, was left out, as he was to be again in Mexico four years later.

How unlucky can you get? Johnny Byrne of West Ham was also omitted, and that struck me as a tragedy. It could have been argued that Johnny, or Budgie as we called him, was the best all-round attacker in England. A lovely lad, Budgie, but he wasn't the most dedicated of footballers. He had a weight problem and dieting bored him. I can see Budgie now on the afternoon that Alf told him the bad news. He had a philosophical smile on his face and a brimming jug of orangeade in his hand!

So we set off to play four matches: Finland, Norway, Denmark and Poland. It was a classic piece of planning. There would be few problems in Scandinavia, so Alf could give everyone a game, assessing his permutations before we met the Poles who would provide the real test.

Jimmy Greaves was soon gleefully knocking in goals, and when we arrived in Kattowice to face Poland, morale was high. One morning I noticed Bobby Moore studying a newspaper with a knowing smile on his face. A journalist who reckoned to have Alf's confidence had suggested that Norman Hunter of Leeds would steal 'Mooro's' place. Norman was a smashing player and marvellously consistent for his club. But Bobby Moore was something else, an opinion that was fully endorsed by Les Cocker, the Leeds and England trainer, who was to die, prematurely, at just fifty-one years old.

Every time Les returned to Elland Road he found himself involved in fierce debates over the respective merits of Moore and Hunter. Les admired Norman and agreed that for a League season, playing week in and week out, he would prefer him. But when it came to international football, there was only one man.

Les put it like this. 'In the dressing room before a game Norman is always prowling about, kicking the wall, all keyed up. Bobby just sits there. Freezer cool. It doesn't matter who you are playing or where you are playing. The buzzer goes and Bobby reaches for the ball as though he's going into the park with his kids. And, of course, when he's up for a game there is no better defender in the world.'

The whole point about Bobby on that tour was that he had been coasting through the easier games, whereas Norman, when he played, was at maximum effort. When he got to Poland, Bobby simply moved up two gears.

Alf's team for that match contained no surprises for the press until the eleventh name was read out. Martin Peters. Prior to that match Martin had played only twice for England and, in fact, didn't turn out for the opening World Cup game against Uruguay. Alf used John Connelly – a left-winger – instead. But Martin's inclusion against the Poles was a clue to the way Alf was thinking. Apart from Connelly, he used his other two wingers, Terry Paine and Ian Callaghan – but he went on to win the World Cup without them.

It was a blazing hot day in Kattowice, so different from the next occasion when I played there for Manchester United in the European Cup. Then the temperature was below freezing! The Poles were always difficult. They were never going to hammer us but this was the final dress rehearsal and we wanted to get it right. If we lost, it would undermine our confidence. It was a hard match. They played possession football, not taking chances to go forward as we did. Then Roger Hunt knocked one in from about twenty yards and I knew we were on our way.

Team spirit was good. We were a family. Even to this day, when we meet, it's like being with brothers. It was a fantastic squad and everyone seemed to have an entirely different personality. Other than Alan Ball, most of us had been around for a long while. We were good pros and strong men. The blend was just about right, the timing perfect. We had won all four games on tour and as we went forward to the finals the record showed that we had lost only one of our previous twenty-two games.

Astonishingly for him, Alf made a public prediction. 'England will win the World Cup,' he said. It was headline stuff and we had to believe it. He clearly did.

6 England *v.* Argentina

World Cup, 1966

I have played in some marvellous places. The Maracana in Rio, looking a trifle tawdry now, but when filled with 200,000 football-daft Brazilians one of the greatest sights on earth; the Bernabeu in Madrid, nestling to one side of a grand avenue in the centre of that splendid city, a monument to the man who founded the club known as Real and named after him; the San Siro in Milan; the Aztec in Mexico City; and Moscow's imposing Lenin Stadium. Closer to home, Old Trafford, Anfield, Highbury and White Hart Lane. And, of course, Wembley. I'll tell you something about Wembley. It's a great place to get a draw!

Quite ordinary teams have held out there against England, the Greeks as recently as March 1983. England got some stick after that match but, believe me, playing at Wembley against opponents who aren't interested in crossing the halfway line can be very discouraging. The reason is the pitch. It might look a picture and I'm sure that Percy Thrower admires the groundsman's work. But try running on it when there is a lot of running to do. After a while it's like moving on loose sand – you feel a gnawing in your calf muscles. Now, imagine playing against a team that is determined to plant bodies across every line of approach, so that you are forced to check, twist and then go again in order to pull players out of position. You are obliged to play along the floor at Wembley, so the build-up is inevitably slow.

I had appeared there often enough before the opening game of the 1966 World Cup to sense that we would do well to

beat Uruguay. We didn't beat them. We drew 0–0, and from
the newspaper reaction you would have thought that England
were out of the competition. In fact, the result didn't depress
us, although we would naturally have preferred to start with
a flourish.

The first game in a World Cup is traditionally a bit of a
bore. Neither team wants to make a mistake and all the
trappings of the opening ceremony tend to overwhelm the
actual event. Alf told us to ignore the critics. We still had to
play Mexico and France in our group and they weren't up
to much. But the nation seemed to have gone sour on us.
Were we going to win the World Cup? No, we weren't. Oh
dear!

The next day we had been invited to Pinewood film studios.
Sean Connery was there making one of the Bond movies and
I remember him coming across to speak while we were having
a buffet lunch. Now, Sean was quite a player in his younger
days and I believe he was on Manchester United's books for
a while. Anyway, he came over and had a right go at the
newspapers.

'They've written you off already,' he growled. 'Bloody hell,
it was only a draw. Forget it.'

There was so much venom in Sean's voice that I began to
fantasize about his 007 role. Didn't he have a licence to kill?
Maybe we should point him in the direction of Fleet Street.

We wouldn't forget that visit to Pinewood because it was
just what was needed. Yul Brynner came in, and George
Segal and Cliff Richard. By the time we left, one or two of
the lads had sunk quite a few drinks. It was a perfect day
and to our surprise Alf allowed us to relax. Maybe he felt
that tension had prevented us from doing ourselves justice
against the Uruguayans. There were five days until we played
Mexico, so it was back to the old routine.

It was soon back to the old routine at Wembley because
the Mexicans left us in no doubt about how they intended to
play. At the kick-off the ball was pushed to a swarthy character called Diaz who immediately thumped it into our

penalty area. But the Mexicans didn't follow up. They went backwards! I got the impression that if trenching tools had been available they would have dug in. We couldn't break them down. Our Kid kept coming up for corners, but although Jack constantly outjumped them, the ball wouldn't break for us. Then, finally, we did it. I got possession deep in our half and when I looked up there was space ahead. Now, I was always taught that if you ran twenty yards at speed with the ball your pursuer would give up. I teach that now. If there is space, use it, unless someone is better placed. Roger Hunt was up ahead and when he saw me coming he set off. Very unselfish was Roger. I kept thinking that I would have to pass if a defender came. But nobody did and that might have had something to do with the defensive posture they'd adopted from the start. I was over the halfway line and still on the move. I dummied one way and found myself about forty yards from goal. That was when the Wembley turf began to work in my favour. What you rarely get there is a bad, unexpected bounce, and when you shoot, the ball usually keeps low. Roger had taken another defender out of my way, so I let fly from twenty-five or thirty yards. When I first started playing for Manchester United, Jimmy Murphy used to say, 'Just bloody shoot. Shoot at the goal. You might miss nineteen times but that twentieth could be the one that will win the match. No crowd will ever criticize you for shooting and missing. But they *will* blast you for not shooting. Don't try to place them. Just get on target. Make sure you hit the goal.'

So now I thought, right. I was nicely in my stride and away the ball went. I knew immediately that the keeper wouldn't get it. An important goal that, and I felt all the frustration of the Uruguay match flooding away. You can sense the public's feeling and I knew what that shot meant to them. Roger got a second and that was it. A draw would have been enough against the French but we beat them comfortably and then the World Cup really began.

We had been watching televised matches from the other

groups and it was plain that Argentina were going to be tough opponents in every sense of the word. They had outstanding players; but it was their hostility that made them so distinctive. Some of their tackling was outrageous and this, combined with the fluency of their technique, made me shudder. Meanwhile a little drama was being acted out behind the scenes.

In the match against France, Nobby Stiles had timed a tackle so badly that Simon finished limping. The French were furious with Nobby and it appears that their anger penetrated the upper echelons of FIFA. It was even suggested in one newspaper that Alf Ramsey might be ordered not to include Nobby against Argentina. I've spent hours defending Nobby, who is a lovely lad and a huge favourite with everyone who knows him. Nobby's eyes weren't too good and he had a reputation as a mean tackler. If he went for the ball he went all the way. Once, when we were in Sweden, Alf was asked how much Nobby weighed. 'I would say about ten stone,' said Alf. 'But when he tackles – ten tons.' That was the way the little fella played and I'm sure he never set out to harm anyone. He could be unbelievably, laughably clumsy. But the world wasn't laughing at him on the eve of the Argentina match. Let Nobby tell the story.

'We were training at Highbury, Arsenal's ground, and I thought it strange when Alf disappeared. Apparently he had been with FA officials who were not happy with me. Alf came back and called me over. He asked if the tackle on Simon was deliberate. I could swear on the Bible that it wasn't. As I went in for the ball, Simon turned. I had already committed myself. Alf believed me. He walked away and when the team was announced I was in. It's been suggested that Alf would have resigned rather than leave me out. I can believe it.'

One report of our quarter final with Argentina the following day suggested that it was not so much a football match as an international incident. Hugh McIlvanney of the *Observer* saw it like this. 'Perhaps the seeds of disorder were present in the situation from the start, for the Argentinians are never the easiest players to discipline. In this tournament they fouled for profit with total cynicism and they showed the familiar delinquent tendency to turn physical if anything displeased or frustrated them.'

I didn't entirely agree because in Chile four years earlier they had shown little of the erupting nastiness that was to typify their attitude in England. South American teams find it difficult to accept the vigorous football they encounter when playing Europeans. Not that they ignore the physical side of the game; it's simply that they go about their work in a different way. The way Argentina went about their work, particularly against us at Wembley, was to scandalize the 1966 World Cup.

There was no doubt in my mind that they presented the most serious threat to our chances, and when we watched them play West Germany I wanted them out of the way. They had Onega, a super midfield player with a great left peg. They had smashing fullbacks – Marzolini was absolutely brilliant. There was Oscar Maz, a devilish little left-winger, and, of course, there was Rattin. They seemed to do everything slowly but they were so strong physically that it was impossible to brush them off. They were always together and they always got the job done. No fair races were allowed. Try to go past them and they would upend you. They spat. They were probably the meanest, roughest team I ever played against.

As it happens, Alf hadn't made much of their behaviour during the pre-match talk, which made his subsequent outburst even more surprising. When it was over, Alf said, 'We have still to produce our best football. It will come against the right type of opposition, a team who come to play football and not act as animals.' I've never understood why Alf said that because it was completely out of character. Having beaten them, whatever the circumstances, it would probably have been better to say nothing. Not that the Argentinians wanted it that way. But let's begin where it began.

I admired Rattin. He was a tremendous footballer, tall, straight-backed and supremely confident on the ball. Arrogant, dominant, he oozed confidence. Had Rattin concentrated on playing football we might not have won the World Cup. But he didn't, and after putting me down on the halfway line, he established a mood that was to consume his team. Down I went again, this time from a blatant trip, and this time Rattin was booked. The atmosphere was now charged with the prospect of scandal and after about half an hour there was a spectacular explosion.

The referee, Rudolf Kreitlein, a German, took another Argentinian name and this so incensed Rattin that he began to pursue Kreitlein, pointing at the armband that signified his captaincy. We were in the same patch at the time and I couldn't take my eyes off him. He was clearly and stupidly trying to run the game. It couldn't go on. Kreitlein stopped, turned and indicated that he was ordering Rattin off the field. All hell broke loose. Argentinians came from everywhere to surround the referee, snarling, spitting, spoiling for a fight.

Curiosity got the better of our younger players. Alan Ball hung around, sniffing on the fringe, a bit naive like Nobby, who looked as though he was about to poke his nose in. On the touchline Alf must have broken out in a sweat that had nothing to do with the heat. Had Nobby taken a faceful of spit, he might easily have reacted and Alf's determined defence of the little man would have backfired.

'Keep away,' I heard Ray Wilson shout urgently. 'Let them get on with it,' and film of that incident shows that his words worked. Rattin had gone to the touchline but he refused to move from there, as if he was trying to argue his way back into the match. For a while it looked as though the match would be abandoned and it seemed ages before we got under way again.

We now had an extra man but it didn't feel like it as the Argentinians emphasized their quality with measured possession football that had us chasing all over the place. Maz began to thrust deep into our half and when he outpaced

George Cohen, it looked a certain goal until Gordon Banks plunged to make a save. We badly needed to score and when we did it was a beauty.

Geoff Hurst had replaced Jimmy Greaves, who was reckoned not to be fully fit. This meant that West Ham had three men in the team and two of them, Hurst and Peters, combined to score a typical 'West Ham' goal: Martin crossed a fine ball and Geoff, attacking the near-post space Martin had aimed for, got the merest touch with his head to beat Roma. We were in front and it finished that way. But down the tunnel there was more to come.

The Argentinians were looking for trouble, cursing us, spitting at us, and it wouldn't have taken much for one or two of the England players to pile in. Alf bundled us into the dressing room and locked the door, but we could hear them outside, kicking, banging, daring us to come out and fight. To this day I think Ray Wilson would have been happy to oblige them.

7   England v. West Germany

World Cup, 1966

You don't expect a rollicking after winning the World Cup. But that's what I got. As though oblivious to the clamour that filled our dressing room, Alf Ramsey really went for me.

'What the bloody hell do you think *you* were doing out there?' he snapped. 'Shooting when you should have been looking around for other people. We should have had it sewn up.'

The reprimand was so severe that for a moment I thought I was back in the Manchester United youth team, listening to Jimmy Murphy! I'd messed up a couple of chances before Geoff Hurst clouted the goal that made us safe, and Alf was still steaming. I began to mumble something about the ball being wet, but Alf was in no mood for excuses; he never was.

There is a picture taken right after Geoff completed his hat trick that captures the explosion of joy on our bench. It's a montage of elated men leaping this way and that; all except Alf. Alf is sitting there, inscrutable, immobile, a professional to the end. He actually told our trainer, Harold Shepherdson, to sit down. I don't believe that Alf was that cool. But having done the job and taken a few knocks along the way, he was suppressing his emotions. That certainly could not be said about the rest of us.

We are all made differently, but I hate it when I see sportsmen crying because they've lost. It makes me suspicious of their temperament and experience has taught me not to rely upon them. But crying when you win! Now, that's a different matter. Sometimes, when I hear an audience respond to an outstanding performance in a stadium or on a stage, tears spring to my eyes and I shed a few that day at Wembley. I shed them for the lads who played and lads who didn't. I got a hug from Jimmy Greaves and I felt for him because he had suffered a huge disappointment when Alf left him out of the final. A lot had been made of that in the press and on TV, but I wasn't astonished by Alf's decision. When Geoff Hurst came in against Argentina when Jimmy was injured, it all began to slot into place. Roger Hunt was a certainty; he was strong, he was tough, he scored goals and he'd run all day. Make no mistake, Roger was an outstanding footballer. He and Geoff suddenly hit it off.

Geoff had learned how to run defenders into bad places and had perfected the knack of checking so that he could receive the ball unmarked. He also had a marvellous understanding with Martin Peters and Bobby Moore, who played with him at West Ham. So, on the one hand, Alf had Hunt and Hurst both of whom could be relied upon to sweat cobs, and on the other Greaves, a fantastic finisher, but a moderate team player. It's been said that Alf showed tremendous courage when he chose to play without Jimmy, but I don't think he saw it that way. He did what he thought was best for the team. Mind you, if we'd lost, Alf would have been condemned for the rest of his days.

Jimmy, of course, didn't play in the semifinal against Portugal, which turned out to be one of the best games in the competition. A smile came back to the face of football that night at Wembley.

I'd played against Benfica a number of times for Manchester United in European Cup ties and friendly matches so I knew a number of their players quite well. Eusebio was incredibly fast and one of the greatest strikers of a ball I'd ever seen. What a thrill that World Cup must have been for him, a poor black boy from the mean streets of Mozambique who had become one of the game's great stars. There was Coluna and Torres, Simoes and Jose Augusto. I mustn't forget him.

Two years earlier on our way home from Brazil, where we'd played in a mini World Cup, the plane refuelled at Recife. The Portuguese players were travelling with us and Augusto approached me in the cafeteria where I was unloading what was left of my cruzeiros, a fistful of grubby notes and tarnished coins. He had a bottle in his hand and it was clear that I was being offered a present.

'Please, for you, Bobby,' he said. It was a brown bottle with a yellow top. I took it and thanked him.

'Isn't that nice?' I said to Ray Wilson.

The Portuguese left us at Lisbon and an hour or so later I woke up feeling parched. The cabin lights were out, there were no stewardesses in the vicinity, so it was Augusto's bottle or nothing. I nudged Ray Wilson to see if he wanted some. 'After you,' said Ray, so I screwed off the yellow top and gulped down what I thought was beer. Beer! It was jungle juice and it nearly took my head off. Pure alcohol. Wait until I got hold of that little so and so! It was a year before I saw Augusto again. And he knew. He knew all right. I raised a hand to my mouth and he collapsed laughing with his mates. As Johnny Byrne would have said, I'd been done like a kipper!

We met again in that semifinal and I got my revenge with two goals. But to emphasize what a sporting match that was, Augusto applauded my second scoring strike. A real nice fella.

Eusebio shot a penalty for the Portuguese – the first goal that we'd conceded – and there were some alarming moments late in the game. But we were through to the final, and even the inscrutable Alf managed a smile.

Two days before the final a few of us were invited to meet Muhammad Ali – or was he still Cassius Clay then? – who was training for a title defence against Brian London. World champion meets the world champions (we hoped). Ali disappointingly had a cold and didn't turn up and there was a hilarious sequel to that back in Fleet Street. The journalist who had taken us to the gym reported Ali's absence to his sports editor, but forgot to tell a colleague who had been detailed to log the Champ's activities. He hadn't turned up either.

With much cunning the sports editor lured his man onto a sucker punch.

'How did Ali look?' he asked.

'Same as usual,' came the reply. 'Danced around. Threw left jabs. Spouted his silly poems. Nothing changes.'

'Yes, it does,' growled the sports editor, triumphantly. 'Ali didn't show up, you lying, lazy sod.'

By then the papers were full of the World Cup final and even Ali had to take a back seat. Reading some of the comments, you would have thought that World War III was about to break out. We'd never lost to the Germans and, pouncing gleefully on the fact one writer began his column like this: 'The Germans, who have never beaten us at their national game or ours . . .' Dear, dear. That was taking things a bit far. And what film did we watch on the eve of the match? *The Blue Max*, with George Peppard as a German air ace in the First World War shooting up British troops on their way to the front! I'm glad the press didn't get hold of that in time.

We respected the Germans but I never thought they could beat us. Uwe Seeler was a terrific centre forward and deadly in the air but he was getting on and I was sure that our Jack could take care of him. I'd played against Helmut Haller when we were both youth internationals and I felt at the time that he was going to be a great player. But he'd got big around the backside and didn't appear to be a threat. Franz Beckenbauer was obviously going to be a star and I was destined to see quite a lot of him. Siggi Held was a good dribbler, unorthodox, quick too, so he worried me a bit.

But we had a good defence. No, a marvellous defence. George Cohen was tough and sharp and I knew from experience that he tackled like a tank. Jack gave nothing away and really understood the game. Bobby Moore was, well, Bobby Moore. Ray Wilson was just about the best left back in the business.

I always shared a room with Ray and he had a list of superstitions that would have foxed Sigmund Freud. I had to pack his boots in our room. He had to carry the bags down. George Cohen had to run about in the dressing room. Players had to be massaged in the same order. Our Jack was always the last.

On the morning of the final I experienced a little flicker of doubt. Not that nervousness which is quite natural on the day of a big game. You wouldn't be a real player if you didn't feel that. No, this was something different. Ray Wilson and I went for a walk, and it was then that I realized how much the game meant to the nation. People kept wishing us good luck, quietly, almost shyly, as though not wanting to unsettle us. Then on the way to Wembley in the team bus we passed Hendon fire station.

The polished appliances were out front, proudly on parade, and burnished bells were ringing for me and my mates. I shivered; if winning the World Cup meant so much to so many people, what if we lost?

There was no hiding place. Wembley would be filled with 100,000 fans and television would beam the match to millions more. It was a new era.

Television had, for the first time, taken so much interest in the World Cup that throughout the competition we'd been able to study the Germans from the comfort of the Hendon Hall Hotel in North London where we were based. As it happens I still use the place, drawn to that suburban hide-away like a homing pigeon. Alf Ramsey did a lot of talking, picking out various points, pinpointing strengths and weaknesses. He didn't go in for dossiers. He expected you to remember what had been said.

The Germans looked strong in midfield, so I was to run with Beckenbauer, Martin Peters with Overath. Nobby, as usual, would be there to pick up the pieces, patrolling in front of the back four. We had various moves worked out to insure against disasters and as long as we kept our heads everything would be all right. Up front we'd take it as it came and see how things went.

When we got to Wembley there were hundreds and hundreds of telegrams piled up in the dressing room, more than we could read, and I was conscious of an unfamiliar hush. There was very little talk as we sorted out our boots, very little of the nervous activity that normally fills a dressing room. Alf moved amongst us, a word here, a word there, and I thought about the Germans. What were they feeling? They couldn't be looking forward to playing us on our own patch. At least, I hoped they weren't.

Then we were out there. Up that slope to a greeting that assaulted the senses. The noise. The colours. The anthems. 'God Save the Queen'. 'Deutschland uber Alles'. A whistle, and we were off and running.

I couldn't believe it when Ray Wilson went for a ball that wasn't there. Siggi Held centred and Ray jumped too early. That wasn't like him. Ray hadn't been caught out since the competition began, and here he was presenting Haller with a chance that was gratefully swept past Gordon Banks. Bloody hell! Ray of all people! A goal down. That wasn't part of the plan.

Haller's goal prompts another Fleet Street tale. Well, they've given us a bit of stick over the years.

We played in red that day, which makes me chuckle whenever I see another white England World Cup winning shirt auctioned at charity dinners. It's the same with the glove that Henry Cooper wore on his left hand when he knocked down Muhammad Ali. I reckon there is a factory turning them out.

Anyway, there was a sports editor who had, for once, abandoned his desk to attend a match. When Haller scored, he stood and cheered. 'What a great start for England,' he cried to his companion. Realizing his error, scarlet with embarrassment, he sat down amidst a stony silence.

It was clear from the start that Beckenbauer had been detailed to trail me as though the Germans had settled for playing ten against ten. They reckoned that Franz was a good enough marker to win the ball from me in areas where his skill would be an instant threat. But he was very young then and I think I had his measure. We scuffled and I passed to Bobby Moore who was fouled. We were about to equalize!

Just prior to that, Tilkowski, the German goalkeeper, had got himself clattered when coming out to challenge Geoff Hurst for a cross and that was to work in our favour. Tilkowski didn't fancy coming off his line after that collision and he was still there when Bobby Moore clipped in a quick free kick. Bobby and Geoff had obviously worked that move many times before for West Ham, and Geoff attacked the space to knock in a marvellous header. He had so much time and room that I looked towards the linesman expecting him to give offside. But the goal stood and we were level.

That was more like it, and when Martin Peters stole in to score in the second half, I couldn't see us losing. We appeared to be the fitter team and there was a little redhead out on the right who never seemed to stop running. In many ways, it was Alan Ball's match. He was only a kid then, alive with enthusiasm for the game, brilliantly endorsing Alf's confidence in him. In fact, I don't think any of us more fully represented the England manager than Alan did. When that World Cup final was over, the German fullback Karl Heinz Schnellinger seemed to have aged ten years. Like a fighter who has forced himself through a supreme test of strength and will, Schnellinger never seemed to be the same again.

But it wasn't over, far from it.

I didn't know how close we were to winning the World Cup in normal time. When I shot wide from Roger Hunt's pass there was only a minute or so left. Were we that close? Then our Jack jumped to head a ball and the referee gave a foul. I thought it was a daft decision but, no matter, we didn't concede goals from free kicks.

Get the wall right. Ensure that there were enough people in there. Does it suit you, Gordon? Nobby pulling and tugging in the line, nervous as though he knew something. Big Emmerich took the kick and tried to drive it through us. The

WATCHING BRAZIL ON TV.

WE SPENT THE FIRST HALF ADJUSTING THE VERTICAL HOLD. THEN WE REMEMBERED Garrincha's LEGS HAPPEN TO BE BENT THAT WAY.

ball flew to the left, Schnellinger got a touch, perhaps with his hand, and Weber, thrusting in on the far post, scored. There must be time left, but there wasn't!

Alf came towards us as we congregated on the halfway line and told us to stay on our feet. 'Don't show them that you are tired,' he said. 'You've won it once, now go out there and win it again.'

As Tommy Banks, that marvellously robust Bolton fullback used to say, 'It were never in doubt.'

So to the goal that will be talked about for as long as England and West Germany play each other at football. 'Ballie' was still running as though we'd only just begun to play, and when he centred from the right Geoff Hurst sent in a ferocious shot that rebounded from the underside of the bar. There would have been no controversy had Roger Hunt done the sensible thing. But instead of finishing things off, he turned away, convinced that Geoff's shot had crossed the line. I was sure that it had but then the referee made his way across to consult the Russian linesman.

I thought, oh no, he's going to disallow it. That isn't fair. It was a goal. I know it was a goal.

After a brief consultation, as the sportswriters say, the linesman pointed to the centre spot and then the Germans went potty.

They've never been convinced that it was a goal, as I discovered in 1982 when the old teams were brought together to play a repeat match. Waists had thickened by then and the tempo was waltz time compared with the urgency that prevailed seventeen years earlier. A bit of nostalgic fun, but afterwards they came at me with the inevitable questions.

'Come on, Bobby,' said the German TV commentator, 'was that really a goal in 1966?'

'Yes,' I replied, 'definitely a goal.' I'm convinced it was, but who can really tell?

The Germans were now forced to throw themselves forward and, don't forget, this was the team that appealed most to their countrymen. It had some special aura which is probably why the defeat that was to come has never been forgotten.

Defeated they were, thrillingly so, beyond all doubt, when Bobby Moore sent Geoff Hurst away with a pass that spread-eagled the German defence. Maybe Geoff thought about running the ball into a corner to waste time. Instead, he ran at the German goal, his strength renewed by some strange energizing force, like a thoroughbred fighting back in the last furlong. He swung his left foot and the ball sped past Tilkowski who once again had remained rooted to his line. We'd done it and Our Kid dropped to his knees and cried.

Most of what happened at Wembley after that remains a blur.

That night there was a great banquet at the Royal Garden Hotel in Kensington to which the four semifinalists had been invited, along with the Prime Minister, Harold Wilson, and a host of other distinguished guests. That too is a bit of a blur, but I remember people presenting me with gifts. Nothing formal. No speeches. A case of port for scoring the most goals against Portugal. Something for something else. Then a suit length. Grey it was. I gave it to Uwe Seeler. I don't know why. Maybe I was embarrassed when he came over to congratulate me. Perhaps I was sorry for him. Anyway I offered him the cloth and he accepted. No mug, that lad. The next time I saw Uwe, he was wearing it!

So we'd won the World Cup and as the night drew on towards another dawn I remembered the drive in from Wembley. Coming through the west side of the city, we'd been cheered by folk of all colours. Black, white, brown, yellow. If winning the World Cup meant that much to all of them, what if we'd lost? It was a chilling thought.

8 Manchester United *v.* Benfica

European Cup final, 1968

Arthur Hopcraft's book, *The Football Man*, published in 1968, contains this splendid passage about Sir Matt Busby:

To watch Sir Matt Busby move about Manchester is to observe a public veneration. He is not merely popular; not merely respected for his flair as a manager. People treat Busby in the way that middle-aged priests of compassionate and sporty nature are often treated: the affection becomes rapidly more deferential as they get nearer to the man. Small boys rush noisily towards him, holding their picture books out for his autograph, and fall silent and shy once they get up close and he calls for less jostling and settles the word 'son' upon them like a blessing. Adults shout his name and grab for his hand. They wave at him in his car.

Those immaculate phrases do not exaggerate Matt's standing in the city for which he fashioned marvellously appealing teams and when a great host sang in acknowledgement of his seventy-fourth birthday at the FA Cup final replay in May 1983, it was movingly clear that he remains synonymous with Manchester United. Many of those supporters were not old enough to have shared in Matt's triumphs, so when he stood to doff his trilby in the Royal Box, I wondered whether they realized how much we owe to a man who, from humble beginnings in a Lanarkshire pit village, became one of the most distinguished and admired figures in the game.

As a result of beating Brighton that evening, Manchester United qualified again for European football, an adventure they could undertake without fear of censure, unlike in 1956 when the Football League were steadfastly opposed to clubs crossing the channel to play competitive matches.

The European Cup had been launched the previous season, but Chelsea, who were champions for the first time in their history, were ordered not to take part. It has become so natural for us to think globally about the game that the League's opposition will now seem strange. In fact, they argued that extra fixtures might seriously disrupt the domestic programme and were still of the same view when Manchester United succeeded to the title. They might have known that Matt would give them a fight.

Sportswriters who referred to Matt as a 'visionary' did so without hesitation because, of all the titles they bestowed upon him, none was more appropriate. Towards the end of the Second World War he took a team to Italy where battleweary troops were entertained by such great players as Joe Mercer, Tommy Lawton, Bryn Jones and Tom Finney; it was then, I suspect, that he saw an unlimited horizon for football.

I was too young fully to appreciate the drama that unfolded at Old Trafford in 1956, but it became obvious from reports in the newspapers that a momentous decision was about to be taken. Matt was determined to lead us beyond the confines imposed by the League and he got his way. It would be twelve years before he captured the prize dearest to his heart and only after great suffering and tragedy.

We shared many experiences during that time and Matt would say, generously, that people spoke of Manchester United and Bobby Charlton in the same breath, but it wasn't until I had become a senior figure both in the United and England teams that I began to know him.

My early years at Old Trafford were spent under the wing of the pugnacious, wise, warm-hearted, incurably sentimental Welshman, Jimmy Murphy, who, as Matt's right-hand man, was responsible for developing the young players who were essential to the club's future. Matt had implicit faith in Jimmy's judgement, so if he showed up on the touchline at a youth match we knew that someone had been brought to his attention.

The public saw Matt as an urbane, avuncular figure, sucking on his pipe, seemingly unmoved by the pressures of management. It was, as he once admitted to a great contemporary, Stan Cullis of Wolves, a deception. I'm told that Matt played that way, calmly, neatly, cleverly concealing his lack of pace with excellent positioning. That deception was maintained in the dressing room, where Matt was never heard to raise his voice however critical the circumstances. He understood, as Alf Ramsey did, that anxious, excitable managers send out anxious, excitable teams. But Matt could be stern. As Nobby Stiles once said, 'If the Boss sent for you, it wasn't to hand out toffees.'

Matt's disapproval seldom surfaced in public, but you knew when he was angry, as Pat Crerand did after one of our games abroad. Paddy had kept us waiting on the bus and as he climbed aboard, clearly embarrassed, Matt spoke up from a front seat.

'You must be a very important person,' he said sarcastically. 'Only an important person could keep the directors, the manager and the players of Manchester United waiting so long.'

A senior member of the team, an established Scottish international, Paddy muttered a sheepish apology and made his way to where we sat.

Apart from being a marvellously creative force, one of the most imaginative wing halfbacks in Europe during the sixties, Paddy was a great chatterer, particularly, as a profoundly committed Catholic, when there were priests about. This respect for the cloth wasn't lost on Denis Law, whose predatory instincts weren't confined to the penalty area.

Paddy was with a priest one day at Stamford Bridge where we were about to play Chelsea, when he saw Denis hovering clearly waiting to be introduced.

'Father, have you met Denis Law?' he inquired of his round-collared friend.

'Delighted to meet you, Denis,' said the priest.

'I'm particularly pleased to meet you,' said Denis.

'And why is that, my son?'

'Well, father, you are the one hundredth priest I have met with Paddy this season.'

Denis, however disarming the smile, wouldn't have dared to try that with Matt. In fact, there wasn't much percentage in trying anything with Matt, who could be, as Maurice Setters once said, one of the hardest men in the game. Maurice, an aggressive wing half who played for us in the 1963 FA Cup final, made this clear one night when speaking to a small group of football writers.

'Don't let Matt kid you,' he said. 'You might imagine he's easygoing. Perhaps a soft touch. But don't ever take Busby on. He's cunning and tough. There isn't a trick he hasn't come across or an excuse he hasn't heard before. You don't take liberties with this fella.'

Maurice's estimate makes Matt's attitude to George Best all the more difficult to explain. When club captain, I found myself ferrying complaints from the other players who were understandably irritated by his extravagant behaviour. Matt should certainly have been firmer with George, although I wouldn't have fancied the job of bringing him into line.

Nothing seemed to work. The rebukes, the coaxing, the fines, the suspensions. George would be apologetic, polite and utterly charming, and to this day he gives Matt full title. But you always knew there would be a next time. Perhaps Matt sensed that George was doomed to a short career, a victim of the self-destructiveness that so often accompanies genius, and simply tried to prolong the act.

Some managers have no stomach for the confrontations that are inevitable when it is necessary to change the team, a weakness that can breed bitterness and mistrust within the club. Matt prepared the ground so that players were often conned into talking themselves out of a place.

This happened to Nobby Stiles. We'd lost at Arsenal and

because things hadn't been going well, Matt had to indicate that he had the situation under control.

'I hadn't been in the team for long and I was still very much in awe of Matt and, of course, I'd grown up with an enormous respect for him,' said Nobby. 'So when he came and sat next to me on the coach as we were leaving Highbury, I felt embarrassed and shy. He asked me how I thought I'd played. I didn't want to sound big-headed, so I mumbled something like "not bad" or "so, so". Matt seemed to agree with that, adding that he was quite pleased with my progress but that a "wee rest" might do me good, because after all it was hard for a young player when the team wasn't getting results. I found myself nodding and Matt left me with an encouraging, fatherly pat. I was dropped for the next game!'

When John Giles, who is Nobby's brother-in-law, heard that story, he shook his head in despair. 'Nobby, you're a mug,' said the Dubliner. 'Matt's tried that one on me. But I always insist that I've played well and he goes in search of another victim.'

Perhaps it was this refusal to accept Matt's ways that led to John's leaving Old Trafford for Leeds, where he became a major force in midfield, responding to Don Revie's more intense style of management. John hadn't experienced that with Manchester United because Matt wasn't a coach in the modern sense, nor was he a tactical innovator. What Matt had, above all else, was a healthy respect for good players and a deep attachment to the beauty and romance of football. In the awful accident at Munich he lost not only fine friends and a great team but the opportunity to influence the direction British football would take. He deplored tactical developments that were bound to smother the individual, and forecast, correctly in my view, that 'too much mind' would rob the game of its more spectacular elements.

Prior to the accident, Matt was working with eighteen players from whom he could select his first team and had been assured by Jimmy Murphy that a fresh crop was coming through. But now those youngsters had to be promoted before

Old Trafford as it was when I still had most of my hair

Just a boy but already the Head Man. Duncan Edwards playing for England against Scotland at Wembley

Sir Matt Busby as he looked three months after the Munich accident; the Boss was still suffering and it showed

The one we waited so long to win – Manchester United, European Champions, 1968

Trying to pierce Benfica's defence during the 1968 European Cup final at Wembley

For an all too brief spell George Best was the world's supreme footballer. I watch as he sets off to score against Benfica

Jimmy Murphy (*front row, left*), the tough but incurably sentimental Welshman who inspired a stricken Manchester United to reach the 1958 FA Cup final. Behind Jimmy at Wembley sits Sir Matt Busby (*second row, centre*) still recovering from the accident

Denis Law – alert, deadly, the man Jimmy Murphy would have bet his life on

If there is a space up ahead, attack it! Going forward for England with Alan Mullery in close support

No one has struck a football harder than this man, Eusebio of Benfica and Portugal, the boy from the mean streets of Mozambique who became a world star

As it should be – Pele and Bobby Moore embrace after Brazil's 1-0 defeat of England during the 1970 World Cup in Mexico

The team Argentina sent to the 1966 World Cup turned out to be the dirtiest I ever played against. Our Kid, my brother Jack, takes a tumble (*above*) and (*below*) referee Kreitlein gets a taste of the trouble that led to Rattin being sent off

The game that meant so much to so many – England *v* West Germany, World Cup final, 1966

Sir Alf Ramsey, a great manager, holds a replica of the World Cup presented to him in 1974

Cry when you win, not when you lose. My brother Jack drops to his knees, overcome by emotion at the final whistle

Seconds left and Geoff Hurst clinches it for England with a history-making World Cup final hat-trick

We are the Champions! Skipper Bobby Moore lifts up the World Cup and I look shattered

There's nothing in football to match the joy of playing. I went on for as long as I could

they had been fully schooled for senior football and Matt, who had rarely been active in the transfer market, was forced to spend. Denis Law, deadliest of close-range finishers, Pat Crerand, Noel Cantwell, Maurice Setters, David Herd and Tony Dunne were all recruited before we won the FA Cup in 1963.

In that year Spurs, with such splendid players as Danny Blanchflower, Dave Mackay, Jimmy Greaves, Cliff Jones and John White, became the first British club to win a European trophy, beating Atletico Madrid 5–1 in the Cup Winners' Cup final.

We knocked Spurs out of that competition the following season but then made a mess of things against Sporting Lisbon. Comfortably placed 4–1 after the first leg, we were wiped out in the return. It was a slack performance and Matt was furious. Hearing a chuckle in our dressing room, he rounded sharply, growling, 'I don't think there's anyone here who's got a reason to feel pleased.' It was enough to restore an embarrassed silence.

Few foreign matches were televised in those days and Matt would set off to study the opposition, strengthening his connections overseas, maintaining the close links he had with great clubs like Real Madrid. There was usually a hilarious sequel because Matt found it difficult to pronounce the names. Eusebio of Benfica came out as 'Yew-see-beeo', and when he referred to another Portuguese star, Jose Luis, as 'Joe Louis', Pat Crerand cracked, 'Aye, he'll pack a punch.' Benfica were always 'Ben-ee-fica', and Hidegkuti, the renowned Hungarian, was 'Hildeguti'.

Nevertheless, Matt had an uncanny memory for names, faces, events, and this, when allied to a natural warmth and the ability to make friends, ensured his lasting popularity. Journalists who might have met him only once were astonished when they were recognized and, in fact, Matt's dealings with the press remain an object lesson to aspiring young managers.

Accessible and cooperative, Matt was also a master of the

verbal body swerve, using it to avoid answering questions that might embarrass him and the club.

'Tell me, Sir Matt, is there anything in this rumour that you are about to buy someone?' a reporter might ask.

'Well, now,' Matt would reply, with much pausing between syllables, employing the old technique because the rumour was probably true.

'Well, now, you see. This can be a difficult game, son, and you have to stay in touch with what's going on. We keep our eyes open, you know. And how is the golf? Are you hitting the ball straight? That's the secret. Keeping it on the fairway.'

By then Matt would be on the move, leaving a bewildered reporter in his wake.

The seasons came and went, and it was a tribute to Matt's initiative that we were continually involved in the quest for honours. FA Cup winners in 1963. Semifinalists in 1964, 1965 and 1966. League champions in 1965. Runners-up in 1964. They were remarkable years because we could never guarantee to play well. Brilliant one week, exasperatingly poor the next, and that was part of the fascination. I had a friend who never missed a match, going to quite extraordinary lengths to ensure that he was always there, simply because he didn't want to miss the incomparable performance of which he was convinced we were capable.

'There's bound to be a game that will matter more than any other,' he said. 'A game that will live for ever in the mind. I would never forgive myself if I missed it.'

Frank McGhee of the *Daily Mirror* dubbed us 'The Team You Can't Trust', and he was absolutely right, but what a marvellous experience. I can remember waking up on the morning of every game at Old Trafford and thrilling to the prospect of playing there in front of a huge crowd. I would sit in the stand after training on a Friday and imagine what it would be like the following afternoon. Compared with what leading footballers earn now, we weren't paid that well, but there was nothing like the excitement of playing for United. If George Best was on song, if Denis Law was in a mood to rattle them in, if I was onto a game, then nobody could stop us. If it turned out to be one of the bad days, then Matt sucked on his pipe and waited for the next time.

But the great prize continued to elude us, and, in 1967, Jock Stein, another outstanding Scottish manager, achieved what Matt had cherished all those years. We were abroad when Glasgow Celtic won the European Cup, beating Inter-Milan in 1967. I felt no envy when the news came from Lisbon; Jock was fully entitled to the tribute paid to him in the dressing room by Bill Shankly of Liverpool.

'John,' he said, using the intimate, correct version of Stein's name, 'you are immortal.' And he was. I wondered if Matt would eventually emulate such a great feat.

We'd gone close in 1966, losing to Partizan of Belgrade in the semifinals, a miserable experience because the Yugoslavs were nothing special and, had we shown our true form, I'm sure that we would have gone on to beat Real Madrid; we conceded two goals away from home and failed to make up the deficit. George Best wasn't fit to play in the second leg, a bristling, bruising affair in which Pat Crerand was sent off after turning on the player who had fouled him.

Paddy was furious and the fact that both men had been sent to the dressing room didn't console him. In a mood to continue the argument, Paddy was frustrated by a locked door, but later that night, at an official reception for the teams, he didn't take his eyes off the offending Yugoslav. He followed him from the table and once outside, a measured walk became a frantic chase into the city streets. That was Paddy finished. Never the fastest of movers, he said, 'Running isn't my game. I had no chance of catching him.'

We'd squandered another chance to win the European Cup, but as champions in 1967, we could try again. Matt remained phlegmatic. He'd had better teams, but perhaps this one would be good enough.

I can see him now, taking his Friday stance on the pitch at Old Trafford, standing to one side of the dressing-room tunnel with Ted Dalton, who, in my opinion, was the best football physiotherapist in the business. Ted didn't just repair damaged tissue. He looked inside your head. No point in trying to kid him. Some players will turn out when it seems that only strapping holds them together. Others will react badly to the slightest twinge. In any case, the decision should never be left to them and it wasn't at Old Trafford. Matt consulted with Ted so that fitness tests were no more than a formality.

It was always the same routine. 'Aye, well, try another sprint and a few wee turns,' Matt would say. 'How does it feel? A bit sore. You'll be all right, son.'

'There's nowt so funny as folk' they say in Yorkshire and that can certainly be applied to footballers. The game is alive with schizophrenics: some of the hardest, meanest, most ruthless tacklers I've come across have been kind, caring people off the field – Nobby Stiles is a classic example – and others who played like lions were sensitive to the slightest physical disorder. Denis Law is in the latter category. Breathtakingly quick reflexes were central to Denis's game and he was never reluctant to go in where it hurts. Jimmy Murphy once said that if he had to select someone to score a goal that would save his life, Denis would be the man. And yet if Denis felt that a muscle or a joint wasn't responding fully to the impulses that flashed from his brain, he might be moodily off colour. At his best Denis was, of course, amazing, so quick, so strong, bursting out of nowhere to score astonishingly from ridiculous angles. He was in hospital, recovering from a knee operation when we eventually won the European Cup and I still find it hard to believe that we managed without him.

It all began uneventfully enough against Hibernians of Malta; then after dealing with Sarajevo of Yugoslavia, we found ourselves in the quarter finals against Gornik, whose skills were supplemented by the toughness you expect in players who have been raised in the Polish coalfields. Their goalkeeper Kostka was sensationally agile and it was an hour before we broke them down at Old Trafford. Law was missing, his knee ominously swollen, and Brian Kidd, who had come off the supply line to take a place in the team, got an invaluable second goal for us in the last minutes. The return leg a fortnight later was played in atrocious conditions: the bus that took us on a two-hour journey from Cracow airport butted through a blizzard, and it continued to snow during the two days we had in which to prepare for the match. The pitch was frozen solid and Matt wasn't keen to risk our slender lead on a surface that would be a constant hazard for defenders. The Poles argued that the game should go on and the Italian referee Lo Bello agreed with them. My mind went back two years, to the day when, giving notice of things to come, England had beaten Poland on the same ground in Kattowice. How different the conditions were on this winter's night. There were times when we were accused of not paying enough attention to tactics that were often necessary in European football. Too arrogant to be negative, some critics suggested.

But we defended well enough that night, chasing and hustling to ensure that the Poles would never outnumber us when it mattered most to them. It was bitterly cold, but we hung on, and despite Lubanski's goal some twenty minutes from time, the hurdle was cleared. We were through, yet again, to the semifinals of the European Cup.

We hadn't looked like Manchester United, not the team that was supposed to thrive on flair, and Matt conceded as much, recognizing, perhaps for the first time in his life, that grim defence, however out of character, was sometimes necessary.

'There is a job of work to do here,' he had said to us. 'So let's do it properly.'

Of all the teams who have fought for the European Cup, none has done more to glamorize the competition than Real Madrid, so when we were drawn to play them it seemed as though destiny was working overtime. They were no longer the Real of di Stefano, Puskas and Kopa, but they still ranked as one of the world's most famous and powerful clubs and a great tradition still ran strong in their blood. That became evident at Old Trafford where, defending magnificently, they restricted us to just one goal, a marvellous effort from George Best that rocketed into the roof of Real's net.

There are few more glorious settings for football than the Bernabeu Stadium in Madrid; set in a fashionable area of that grand city, its shape, on the inside, gives the impression of sheer cliffs reaching up towards some mysterious lost world in the night sky.

If Gento continued to arrow with disconcerting swiftness along Real's left flank, Pirri and Amancio could do damage elsewhere, and the Spaniards would be encouraged to believe that they were more than capable of putting us out.

Concentrate, keep your head, don't give the ball away. We carried those thoughts with us onto the field. Forty-five minutes later we were losing 3–1! Was our world crumbling again? We slumped on seats in the dressing room. It was then that Matt revived the dream.

To begin with he altered our tactics, sending David Sadler forward from the auxiliary defensive role he was given in the first half; then he began to encourage us, speaking calmly as though dealing with children who had lost their way.

'Go back out there with your heads up,' he said. 'We aren't losing three-one, because George scored at Old Trafford. There's only a goal in it, so don't give up hope. Play your football. Let's attack!'

Just before we went back out I heard Matt say, 'It's a funny old game this. Anything can happen. We need only one goal to force a replay in Lisbon or somewhere.'

The half-time interval can work both ways. The team that has been on top often struggles to take up the initiative again because they have been told to guard against a renewed surge by the opposition. This certainly seemed to be the case with Real who simply weren't the same team in the second half. It wasn't that we began to play well or that we were creating chances, but they weren't dangerous any more. The pace had slackened and for the first time in the match we looked tidy.

Then David Sadler scored. Not a great goal. Pat Crerand

sent over a free kick, Bill Foulkes headed on, and David's shot, half hit and no more than hopeful, crept past the keeper. We were overjoyed. A replay. At least a replay.

Real's counterattack lacked conviction, and from experience I could sense that their supporters were growing anxious. As I went to collect the ball for a throw-in, one of them reached out and grabbed it. I told myself to stay cool. I sauntered across and the man put the ball meekly in my hand as though accepting that we would go through.

I was fifty yards behind the play when George Best slithered past two men and made for goal, so it was impossible to support him. Others were trying, among them, astonishingly, Bill Foulkes who, inspired by some inner conviction, had abandoned his position in defence. Bill just kept on going, no one picked him up, and when the ball came across he knocked it into the net. Some 10,000 people had followed us to Madrid and they went berserk, but none more so than Denis Law who sprang from his seat on the trainer's bench as though leaping for a cross. There was a roof overhead and Denis gave himself a painful, almost concussive crack!

When the final whistle went, I felt as I had done at the end of the World Cup final. As far as I was concerned we'd won the European Cup. How could we fail to win it after all we'd been through that night? It was an emotional moment and there were tears in our eyes when Matt and I embraced.

Because of his extraordinary feats for Portugal in the 1966 World Cup, it had become fashionable to look upon Eusebio as the new Pele. The black, lithe Benfica forward probably generated more power than any of his contemporaries. He was also murderously quick. But he wasn't in Pele's class.

Given adequate support, Pele was almost impossible to mark. He invented ways of playing the game, gymnastically defying the restraints opponents tried to impose upon him. Eusebio, much more of an individualist, was easier to contain and his temperament was suspect. I worried a bit about Eusebio before we met Benfica in the European Cup final at

Wembley, but Pele would have been the source of sleepless nights.

Eusebio was bound to threaten us and that meant giving him to Nobby Stiles, who had done a marvellous job against Portugal in the World Cup semifinals. I was confident that the little man would be no less successful in the colours of Manchester United. Alan Ball must have thought so as well.

'That Eusebio is a PR [public relations] player,' Alan used to pipe during the World Cup. 'He's always shaking hands, always clapping the other team. It's a con. He wants to be everybody's friend. Sort him out, wee man.' Nobby had no friends on the pitch!

Benfica had other excellent players. Coluna, a vastly experienced and cunning wing half, was a great influence in midfield; Jose Augusto was still an exceptional forward; and Torres was aptly named. Translated, Torres means 'tower'. A very tall man, he used his height to full advantage, both when heading for goal and when sending the ball to the feet of others. Simoes, the left-winger, was scurryingly quick and combative.

We considered their various talents at a hotel in Surrey where Queen Elizabeth I had once stayed, a quiet, relaxing place, far from the excitement that was building up in the land. We marvelled at Lester Piggott's prowess as he brought Sir Ivor home in the Derby and then we set off for Wembley. We weren't just playing for Manchester United, but for England, and the whole of Europe was aware of what this one match meant to Matt Busby.

It was significant that only three of the men who played for us that night – Pat Crerand, Tony Dunne and Alex Stepney – had been transferred from other professional clubs. The lads who had played in Europe a long time all seemed to be there: Bill Foulkes, Shay Brennan, little Nobby. Then there were the younger ones, Johnny Aston and Brian Kidd. They were Manchester lads, so they knew what was expected of them. They had grown up with it all. Brian Kidd would have been going on ten years old at the time of the Munich accident.

Now it was his nineteenth birthday, symbolic that, because Manchester United's reputation had been built on youth.

It was a humid evening, not the best conditions for football, and I was conscious of an untidy, nervous start. Neither team could get going and free kick followed free kick with numbing regularity. The game was quite nasty at times and I mouthed my disapproval when Eusebio, coming in late at Pat Crerand, wickedly thrust a boot over the ball.

The only encouraging feature of our play at that stage was the ease with which Johnny Aston sped past Benfica's right back, Adolfo. I felt that if such superiority could be maintained in the second half, we'd really get amongst them. I could not have foreseen what was soon to occur.

Heading wasn't exactly the strongest element in my play. I left that to others, particularly Denis Law and George Best, who for comparatively short men were quite sensational in the air. So it must have come as a shock to my family, my friends, my team-mates, Matt Busby, Jimmy Murphy, Benfica and the world at large when I headed David Sadler's cross past Henrique. Seeing David out wide, I made for the near post, hoping to drag a defender out of position so that there would be more space for someone else to connect with the cross. Still on the move when the ball dropped short, I rose and glanced it on without breaking stride, and it went just inside the far upright. No goal has given me greater pleasure.

Johnny Aston was given a lot of the ball after that because he was in top form and continued to get past Adolfo, but Coluna began to draw Benfica together, and when Torres outjumped our defenders to send a terrific pass downwards, Graca raced in to equalize.

The World Cup final, those tormenting last minutes of normal time during which the Germans drew level, had made me more aware of the clock, and I was already preparing myself for a further punishing half hour at Wembley when I saw Eusebio bearing down upon our goal.

Alex Stepney moved to meet the danger and then scuttled

back, sensing that he'd left his line too early. Perhaps that unsettled Eusebio, who, instead of taking his time, blasted the ball at our net. Fortunately for us, Alex had made himself as tall as possible, standing right up, so that in Eusebio's eyes he must have filled the goal. The ball stuck in his hands. It was a remarkable save, but one that was only possible because Eusebio went for a spectacular goal instead of settling for the simple thing. Pele would have scored.

Extra time. It was the World Cup all over again; only the faces of those lying on the ground around me were different.

Matt busied himself amongst us. 'You are not playing your football,' he said. 'Stop giving the ball away. Benfica are shattered. Look at them. We are in much better shape. We've got this far, now let's finish it.'

The Portuguese certainly did seem to be in a bad way, as if Eusebio's miss had demoralized them, and it went through my mind that we were better equipped for this sort of thing than they were. Benfica sank even lower when poor Adolfo, who had been tormented by Johnny Aston, then allowed a clearance from Alex Stepney to slide beneath his outstretched foot, straight to George Best. George was off, giving a fair imitation of Wembley's electric hare, supremely confident, doing ultimately what he always expected of himself in such situations. When George got away like that, goalkeepers were inclined to feel that they had chosen the wrong career and I'm sure Henrique was no exception. George's shoulders twitched, he flicked his hips and planted the ball into an empty net before wheeling away, a hand held high in triumph. Eusebio had been shown how it was done.

Benfica baffled me because they hadn't attempted to alter their tactics, doing nothing to try to solve the problems presented by Johnny Aston who continued to carry the ball past them, running on to the corner, putting the length of the pitch between him and our goal. It was the best possible way to waste time.

We needn't have worried. Henrique, who struck me as being too small for the job, could only push out Brian Kidd's header and Brian headed the ball back into the net. It was all over, and I completed the scoring when I got a satisfying touch to Brian Kidd's pass.

Suddenly everyone was clamouring for Matt as he came from the bench to embrace us. What images must have flashed through his mind. Duncan Edwards, powering forward with the ball at his feet; Eddie Colman shimmying this way and that; the near oblivion of a Munich airstrip. I am familiar with those images.

As the excitement began to subside I felt very tired and a bit sick. There was a reception at Wembley but it was too much for me; I needed air. In the tunnel below I discovered Pat Crerand, who was also suffering. The carpets that had been rolled out for royal guests were already pushed to one side and we sat on them, not saying a word.

The club had arranged a big dinner at the Russell Hotel in London to which all the old players and the relatives of those who had died at Munich were invited. When I failed to show up, it was suggested that I was unable to handle the emotion of it all. That wasn't the case. My wife, Norma, went downstairs to join the party, but whenever I tried to follow her the nausea welled up inside. After nearly passing out at the top of the stairs I went back to our room and slept.

They were all there that night. Johnny Berry, Kenny Morgans – all the people I wanted to see. I didn't even see them the following morning because I had to leave the hotel at 8 a.m. to join the England party who were leaving for the European championships.

Norma told me that it had been a marvellous night, a tearful one too, with Matt singing 'What a Wonderful World'. He was entitled to do that.

9 England *v.* Colombia and Ecuador

Pre-World Cup tour, 1970

If there was a World Cup for pickpockets, Colombia would walk over. They've got the most accomplished thieves on earth; audacious, ingenious and very often deadly. Fagin wouldn't have got into the reserves.

In the more remote regions of that spectacularly contoured country, ferocious bandits operate with such chilling efficiency that, in one year alone, they were reckoned to have been responsible for 12,000 murders. Not the most inviting of places, so I wasn't exactly thrilled at the prospect of playing there for England in 1970 as we prepared to defend the World Cup in Mexico.

Jimmy Greaves, who drove in the World Cup Rally, was told to put his foot down when he reached Colombia. In view of what occurred, I wish we'd done the same.

Colombia, or, to be more precise, the capital city, Bogotá, already had an infamous connection with British football, the source in 1950 of a major poaching scandal that involved some of our leading players, including Neil Franklin, a brilliant centre half. Neil's international career was effectively ruined in Bogotá and another equally notable England defender was soon to find himself in similar peril.

To rationalize our fears about playing at intimidating altitudes, Alf Ramsey had arranged a brief tour of Colombia and Ecuador that would also enable him to trim six players from the squad of twenty-eight who set forth from England that summer. We spent two weeks quietly acclimatizing in Mexico City, 'catching our breath', as one writer put it, at 7500 feet!

Then we began to climb towards Bogotá and Quito, where Alf had set up matches for both 'A' and 'B' teams. We were heading for trouble. That relatively simple exercise was to become the stuff of which front pages are made.

Even before leaving our pleasant quarters I had a sense of foreboding. Not that there was anything wrong within the squad. Team spirit was, as ever, excellent and I felt that we were better equipped than in 1966, good enough, in fact, to emulate Brazil, the only country to win the World Cup on a continent other than their own.

Gordon Banks looked unbeatable. Francis Lee, an aggressive and imaginative forward, was in peak form. Keith Newton, Terry Cooper and Tommy Wright had become outstanding fullbacks. Alan Mullery was full of himself in midfield and couldn't wait to get to grips with Pele. Why, then, did I experience that tremor of apprehension? Mainly, I think, because we were about as popular with the Mexicans as an outbreak of typhoid!

As the reigning world champions we attracted considerable commercial interest. There had been no shortage of companies eager to supply our needs and, quite naturally, they wanted to advertise their cooperation. The Mexicans are a proud people, so when it was revealed that we were bringing our own bus, our own water, even fish fingers, they were clearly insulted. Enraged editorials accused us of being aloof and snobbish. Did we think that they had yet to discover the wheel and the internal combustion engine? If their water was good enough for the President of the United States when he visited them, what right had we to assume that it was running with bacteria?

One of our own reporters, who allowed himself to be interviewed in an attempt to smooth things over, was described in a fierce and wickedly biased article as being, 'like the English players, a long-haired, drunken pirate'. Later that day, in the Press Centre, he had to be pulled off the offending author.

Alf, for whom I retain the utmost respect as a football

manager, was partly to blame because he paid little or no
attention to public relations and failed completely to take the
sensitivity of our hosts into account. I know that he had been
unhappy with the transport which had been made available
to us in Mexico the previous summer, a cramped, scruffy,
airless bus that barely made it to the match. But was it really
necessary to ship out one of our own, particularly as none of
the other countries went to such an extreme?

Sportsmen, in common with all travellers, are vulnerable to
debilitating stomach disorders and Mexico offers a ferociously
virulent type, described locally, with bleak humour, as
'Montezuma's Revenge'. Dr Neil Phillips, the team physician,
took every possible care to ensure that we weren't struck
down – one of us would be and in desperate circumstances,
but more of that later – and we disobeyed his rules at our
peril. Plain food. No ice in the soft drinks. Bottled water in
the rooms. I'm sure that most of the other teams were just
as careful, that the Italians and the West Germans brought
out their own rations. The difference was that, foolishly, we
publicized the fact.

Then there was Alf's uneasy relationship with the press
and television. He was a football man, pure and simple. All
his energy was devoted to the preparation of the England
squad and its welfare. He didn't court the cameras. He wasn't
approachable outside the tightly knit confines of the party.
Most of our press lads had grown used to Alf, even if few of
them could claim to have his confidence. But the Mexicans,
with their understandable appetite for news about a World
Cup being played in their homeland, simply couldn't come
to terms with his nature. When asked if he'd been introduced
to Jose Werneck, a prominent Brazilian journalist, Alf replied,
'Yes, he's a pest!' Alf was suspicious of foreigners and it
always showed.

After we'd played Mexico in the Aztec Stadium in 1969, a
posse of Mexican reporters clattered into our dressing room.
Alf, furious at this intrusion, immediately threw them out,
much to the amusement of the British press, who had been

brought up to accept that the England dressing room was out of bounds. When a truce was finally agreed upon Alf was asked if he had anything to say.

'Yes, there was a band playing outside our hotel at five o'clock this morning. We were promised a motorcycle escort to the ground. It never arrived. When our players went out to inspect the pitch they were abused and jeered by the crowd. I would have thought that the Mexican public would have been delighted to welcome England. But we are delighted to be in Mexico and the Mexican people are wonderful.'

The final sentence of that statement, carrying as it did the suggestion of a hurried afterthought, indicated that Alf was trying. But when it came to public relations, he could never bring himself to try hard enough. The concession was always made grudgingly.

It was the Brazilians who showed us how it should be done. In Guadalajara, where we would meet in Group 4, they mounted a hugely successful propaganda campaign that seduced the Mexicans, sending players on visits to local hospitals, staging parties for poor children, showering them with badges, flags and autographed booklets. Conditioned as we were to the pompous posture adopted by The Football Association – note the 'The' – we all felt that it was a bit theatrical. Maybe so, but the Brazilians won massive support for their cause, while we continued to arouse unmistakable hostility.

So we left for Bogotá, amused for a moment by the horror that registered clearly on Nobby Stiles's face when he realized that we were being carried by an Argentinian airline.

'It's a plot,' muttered Nobby, remembering not only that infamous World Cup tie in 1966, but the shame of being sent off when playing for Manchester United against Estudiantes of Buenos Aires in the World Club championship. 'We'll never be seen again. You've got to believe it.'

A long, sweaty trip ended uneventfully on the steps of the Tequendama Hotel, one of those cloned high-rises that have sprung up all over the world.

There was a curfew in Bogotá and we were warned that

even when moving round during the day, it was advisable to stay in large groups. Pedlars were everywhere, appearing to come out of the walls, offering watches, rings, brooches, diamonds, and anyone careless enough to dangle an arm out of a car window was odds on to be robbed. That actually happened to one of our officials when the vehicle in which he was travelling was held up at traffic lights. He wound down the window to get some air, and in a flash his watch had gone. No point in giving chase. The thief had fled.

We confined our window shopping to the hotel arcade, which is how Bobby Moore came to be involved in something so sensational that his great career could easily have been damaged beyond repair.

After wandering around, admiring clusters of ferociously priced emeralds, we ended up in a tiny shop, the Green Fire, little more than a kiosk, near the main reception desk. I asked the girl who worked there if I could see a necklace that was locked away in a cabinet – everything was – and she opened the case. It was priced at £6000, enough to send me reeling towards the door. There were no bracelets on view.

We were sitting outside, wondering what to do next, when the shop assistant appeared and asked Bobby to stand up. She spoke in Spanish, and began rummaging beneath the cushions, moving them around. We didn't understand. Maybe something was wrong with the settee. Perhaps we shouldn't have been sitting there. A man arrived and began to make a fuss. He said there was a bracelet missing, and we looked at him in amazement. Then I realized what they were suggesting. The girl continued to fiddle with the cushions, as though expecting to find something.

The situation was obviously becoming serious, so we decided to send for Alf. He eventually arrived with an interpreter and the hotel manager, who confirmed that Bobby was being accused of stealing a bracelet.

I leaped to his defence. 'Look,' I said, 'I was in the shop with him and there wasn't a bracelet in sight. We didn't see any bracelets.'

Then the police came to take Bobby away, leaving our officials to contact the British Embassy. I couldn't believe it. This couldn't be happening. On the other hand, Bobby hadn't taken anything, so what was the point of worrying?

I was convinced that a mistake had been made and that the bracelet would eventually reappear. Then I turned cold. What if they'd accused me? Why hadn't they accused me? Maybe it was because I had been standing near the door of the little shop. Bobby Moore had been closer to the counter.

But why wasn't I pulled in? They hadn't found anything on Bobby Moore, so why hadn't they searched me? I was sure that they would admit it had been a terrible mistake. But they didn't. Was it a plot? Had someone set out to discredit us?

Alf was stunned, confiding to the handful of reporters who were aware of the incident that nothing worse had happened to him during seven years as England's manager.

We won our matches – the senior team's 4–0 victory strengthening the belief that there was unlikely to be a better organized or more spirited outfit in Mexico – and when Bobby, who played, was allowed to travel with us to Ecuador, it seemed as though his problem could be dismissed as a minor embarrassment.

Quito was where we finally came to terms with the altitude, playing at 9300 feet, chests frighteningly tight, hearts pounding, our lips flecked with foam. There wasn't much urging on done during the games that were won there that day. Alan Mullery was unusually muted; so was Alan Ball. They had no energy to spare. When Mullers tried to shout, all that came out was a gurgle! It was hard but satisfying. We came through the pain and conquered our fears. We were returning to Mexico with a substantial bonus.

By then Alf had jettisoned six players. Four of them – Peter Shilton, Bob McNab, Ralph Coates and Brian Kidd – had elected to go home. Peter Thompson, so unlucky to suffer a repeat of his experience in 1966, and David Sadler had taken up Alf's offer to stay with us.

I felt for them all, as I did for Alf who, responding perhaps to the discretion displayed by those informed few who had not reported Bobby Moore's dilemma, allowed himself to be compromised. Astonishingly, in view of his normal intransigence, he succumbed to the pleas of Sunday newspapermen who were keen to vault the time difference that separated them from their deadlines. The deal was that secrecy would be maintained until Alf had informed the players, an embarrassing task that had to be undertaken before the story appeared.

He was betrayed by a sports editor in Manchester, who, not content with the news and astonishingly ignorant of the speed with which international telephone calls can be made, sent a reporter to seek out David Sadler's wife. She rang David, and Alf found himself confronted with bitter, justifiable complaints from men who clearly felt that they had been let down. In normal circumstances this would have led to an irreparable rift between the England manager and the press. But Alf's mind was elsewhere. It was in Bogotá.

The Bobby Moore case still hadn't been resolved and we were due to pass through Bogotá *en route* to Mexico City. On the morning of our departure from Quito I could sense Alf's nervousness. I'll never know why we went back to Bogotá, or indeed why we should revisit the Tequendama Hotel, but as we sat down to watch the film *Shenandoah*, Bobby was approached in the darkness and led away.

Even then we believed that he would show up at the airport. When he didn't, I went to Alf and offered to stay. I'd been with Bobby. Surely I could help. But Alf ordered me onto the plane and then boarded it himself, to sit impassively in his seat, looking straight ahead. Dr Andrew Stephen and Denis Follows, the chairman and the secretary of the Football Association, were left behind in Bogotá to support our embassy in their efforts to get Bobby released. Going into Panama, we had to pass through a violent electric storm that would normally have made me tremble. But I just kept thinking about Bobby. We had a couple of hours to stretch our legs in Panama airport, and Alf kept on the move, as though trying to avoid a conversation with anyone.

Once again I wondered how I would have reacted in Bobby's predicament. To be quite honest, I wouldn't have weathered it as well as he did. He is, of course, immensely cool, and that characteristic worked for him during the week he spent under house arrest. I would have been demanding answers, trying to hurry things up. But Bobby stayed calm, reacting as he would in a crowded penalty area.

By the time we reached Mexico City news of Bobby's arrest had already broken and there appeared to be thousands of reporters and cameramen at the airport. Some of them didn't fail to spot Jeff Astle, who was slumped in a chair, a raincoat draped over his lolling head to conceal the fact that he'd been drinking. Jeff is an extremely nervous flier, and when a few large scotches were mixed with the tranquillizer that he'd taken in Bogotá, the result was quite dramatic. I hate to think of the wrath that would normally have been heaped upon Astle by our manager, but Alf forgave him, recognizing no doubt that his own preoccupation with Bobby Moore had led to a lapse in discipline.

The Mexicans were not about to be as generous. In the following day's newspapers we were accused of wholesale drunkenness, nonsense of course, but inevitable in view of their hostility. During the days that followed I inquired repeatedly about Bobby. Then, when we got to Guadalajara to luxurious quarters at the Hilton Hotel, the news began to improve. The case against him had begun to collapse because of wildly conflicting evidence, and it appeared that public opinion in Colombia was firmly behind our captain. When writing in the Mexican sports paper *Esto*, a former manager of Brazil, Joao Saldanha, revealed that footballers from the Brazilian clubs Santos and Portuguesa had suffered similar embarrassement in Bogotá. He had himself, many years previously, been accused of theft when playing for Botafogo, discovering with the help of a policeman that the missing jewel had been placed in a back room of the shop. Saldanha

concluded by declaring Bobby Moore to be an honourable man.

Bobby's absence did, without doubt, have a profound effect upon the squad. It wasn't that he was particularly close to any of us. But his stature was immense and had he not played in that World Cup, had he been held in Bogotá, the effect on morale would have been so damaging that it is doubtful that we would have progressed so far.

But Bobby Moore did play, returning from Bogotá to make a huge impression on the hundreds of reporters who were waiting to interrogate him in Guadalajara. The entire England squad turned out, applauding him into the Hilton, and I believe that there was the merest trace of moisture in his eyes. But only for a moment, and I recall someone saying that Bobby Moore would be the last man he would want to play against in that World Cup!

10   England v. Brazil and West Germany

World Cup, 1970

No one did more than Gordon Banks to nourish the belief that we could retain the World Cup in Mexico. Gordon was phenomenal in 1970, not only the best goalkeeper in the world, but probably the most important player in the competition.

Helmut Schoen, the West German manager, was a confirmed Banks fan, so was Mario Zagalo of Brazil; a student of Voodoo, he might well have been found thrusting large pins into a Banks effigy. If that was indeed the case, it might explain the sickness that was soon to strike our man down.

I recall Malcolm Allison saying that if the goalkeeper is playing well, he raises the game of the players in front of him, but that if he plays badly, the team will probably lose regardless of how other players perform. Well, we always knew what to expect from Gordon and it was immensely encouraging to have a man behind us who never seemed to make a mistake. He was alert, incredibly agile and his concentration was flawless. There were times when Gordon had very little to do, but if a crisis suddenly arose, he was on his toes.

None of us can be sure when we are at the absolute peak of our powers, that brief period of fulfilment that precedes the inevitable downhill run. But that, surely, is where Gordon was in 1970. He got through an incredible amount of work in training, making utterly remarkable saves. Many managers prefer not to use their goalkeepers for target practice but Alf

Ramsey would have needed a tractor to drag Gordon from the practice ground.

Gordon will always be remembered for the save he pulled off against Brazil, plunging backwards to reach a header that Pele had directed viciously downwards, diverting the ball over his crossbar with a miraculously timed scoop. I said it then and I have no hesitation in repeating myself now, it was, without doubt, the greatest save I have ever seen.

But much occurred before Gordon was able to demonstrate his brilliance in such an arousing fashion, most of it in the immediate proximity of the Guadalajara Hilton where we were based for Group 3 games against Rumania, Brazil and Czechoslovakia. I have already mentioned the hostility we encountered in Mexico that summer, the result of clumsy promotional ventures and totally inadequate public relations.

On our return to Mexico City from Bogotá we were branded as drunkards and thieves and the reception in Guadalajara proved to be just as unfriendly. The sight of a Union Jack was enough to provoke a torrent of abuse and Brazilian flags flourished everywhere. When we strode out to play against Rumania on 2 June the locals made it abundantly clear who they were pulling for. As someone wrote at the time, the easiest way to be popular in Mexico was to play against England.

Corporate television was calling the tune by then and, in order to provide European viewers with live coverage, we found ourselves kicking off at high noon, a disgraceful arrangement in view of the heat and humidity that was soon to descend upon us.

In that respect the Rumania match turned out to be a relatively comfortable experience, the temperature less cruel than it had threatened to be, and we were glad of the rain that fell before the end. Neither did the altitude – Guadalajara is at 5212 feet – prove to be an insurmountable problem, a tribute to the thoroughness of Alf Ramsey's planning. The punishing work done higher up in Colombia and Ecuador was paying off.

The first match you play in a World Cup is bound to be a problem as we had discovered against Uruguay in 1966. You are keen to make a good start but there is an inhibiting awareness that things could so easily go wrong. They didn't, although we had some anxious moments before Bobby Moore, fully recovered from his disturbing experience in Bogotá, began to play with an admirable authority that confirmed he was the finest central defender in the world.

I don't know what was said in Rumania's dressing room during the interval, but their left back Mocanu began the second half as though he was on a bonus for breaking legs. We had barely restarted when he cut down Keith Newton so viciously that our man had to go off. Tommy Wright came on for Keith in time to see Francis Lee become Mocanu's next victim. Mocanu's mood spread throughout the Rumanian team and some perturbed fidgeting was being done on our bench.

A goal was needed to settle things down and we got one when Alan Ball's high centre reached Geoff Hurst. The ball fell nicely for Geoff and he was able to slide it through the goalkeeper's legs. Hardly a classic but good enough.

Not that it did anything to persuade Mocanu that there wasn't much profit in kicking Englishmen. He simply looked around, selected another target and this time it was Tommy Wright who went down in pain.

There had been much talk of firm refereeing and the opening match between Mexico and Russia at the Aztec Stadium had been notable for the number of bookings. But Vital Loraux, the Belgian who handled our game, was so passive that those who had forecast a violent World Cup had every reason to believe that their calculations were accurate.

A Siberian internee was likely to be granted more free time than the England footballers who played for Alf Ramsey ever got, so it came as a pleasant surprise when we were permitted to take a relaxing drink in the Hilton bar that evening. We were pleased with the result, if not entirely with our performance, but there was the usual banter. Alan Mullery was full of it, gleefully recording how he had got the better of Lucescu in a heated personal exchange.

'I whacked him, then he whacked me. Later on I got to him again and his boot came off. He swore in my face, so I smiled and said, "When you going home then? June the fifteenth?" '

That would be the witching hour for the teams who failed to qualify in their groups. With a victory under our belts, we were confident of going forward with Brazil.

Brazil now began to occupy our thoughts. How good were they? Was the great Pele truly a rejuvenated force? What tensions existed in their camp? They had recently changed managers, replacing the controversial Joao Saldanha with Zagalo, who had played as a scuttlingly effective all-purpose left-winger in their World Cup winning teams of 1958 and 1962. Would Zagalo impose his functional nature upon the team or would he allow their marvellous natural talent to flourish?

Answers were soon available against Czechoslovakia in the Jalisco Stadium the following day where it was immediately evident that Zagalo had laid a steadying hand on his country's football. Far from adopting the winged 4-2-4 system that was eagerly claimed for them by some of our less knowledgeable writers, Brazil used Rivelino on the left side in midfield and Pele as a foraging inside forward. Little Tostao, mercifully recovered from the eye injury that had jeopardized his career, could be found further upfield, and Jairzinho, a winger whose build suggested that he might offer a convincing challenge for the middleweight championship of the world, ran with alarming directness along the right flank.

Rivelino's first contribution was a disconcertingly stacatto dribble, leading to a raking centre that Pele sent fractionally wide. Stunning stuff, which hinted that this might indeed be one of Brazil's great teams.

A popular misconception is that Brazilian players are not schooled, that their game is allowed to remain pure, their dazzling teamwork a product of endless games played on the beaches of Rio. But, believe me, they think deeply about the game. Anyone who has watched matches in the Brazilian leagues will also be aware that the tackling is no less severe than it is elsewhere in the world. Nevertheless, some concern had been expressed about the quality of Brazil's defence and those fears seemed to be justified when Petras put Czechoslovakia in the lead. Whipping the ball away from a hesitant Clodoaldo, he ran on with a refreshing, unfussed swiftness to belt it over Felix's right shoulder. When Adamec then went close following an appalling error by Carlos Alberto, the drumbeats took on a more sombre note.

We had been warned about Brazil's free kicks, not only the swerving, dipping trajectory of their shots, but the cunning ploys that were used to set them up. Skilled dribblers were sent to invite tackles on the edge of the penalty area and no one was better at gaining an advantage there than Pele. When a defender was punished for bringing him down, we waited expectantly for the outcome. We were not disappointed.

Six Czechs gathered between the ball and their goal, scrambling into place as first Gerson, then Pele, shaped as though about to shoot. While this was going on Jairzinho strolled onto the left-hand side of the Czech wall. My eyes were on Rivelino, who was standing innocently at right angles to the activity. Now he launched himself at the ball, striking a violent left-footed shot straight at Jairzinho, who flung himself aside. The ball flew on and found the net, just brushing the goalkeeper's fingertips on the way.

I looked at Martin Peters and we exchanged grimaces. Alf Ramsey muttered something to his assistants, Harold Shepherdson and Les Cocker. Bobby Moore was lost in thought.

Brazil scored three more goals to win as convincingly as we had thought they would. In four days' time it would be our turn.

Pausing to speak with a friend in the lobby of the Hilton Hotel later that evening, Alf Ramsey expressed his concern.

'My Christ, these people can play,' he said. 'And we shall have to do something about their free kicks.'

In the meantime Bobby Moore had begun to apply himself to the problem and when we trained at the Atlas sportsground the following day he presented Alf with a solution.

'Let me stand behind whoever tries to muscle into our wall,' he said. 'As long as I hold my ground, I should be able to block the shot.' Bobby was to do more than that.

We were to face Brazil on the Sunday, and in the hours leading up to the match, Guadalajara was alive with speculation. Defeat would not eliminate us from the competition; on the other hand, a victory would cement the belief that we were good enough to beat anyone.

There were many familiar faces in town. Don Revie and Joe Mercer were there to work for television and we were visited by a collection of famous British players who had been brought out by a magazine. Billy Bremner, John Giles, Charlie Cooke, Terry Hennessey, Gary Sprake and an ebullient Tommy Docherty. Welsh, Scots and Irish, they were with us to a man, emphasizing the comradeship that exists despite national differences in our game.

In the moment that we won the World Cup in 1966, Denis Law, a committed Scot, was approaching the eighteenth green at a golf club in Cheshire.

'England have won!' called someone excitedly from the steps of the clubhouse.

'Bastards,' snarled Law, playing the part well.

We detected no animosity in the footballers who came to watch us in Guadalajara. But the streets around our hotel were alive with hatred. On the Friday and Saturday nights, hordes of Brazilians and Mexicans clamoured incessantly beneath the windows of our rooms, making it impossible to sleep. They kept up a constant din, driving around the hotel, horns blaring, flags waving. When we looked down there wasn't a policeman in sight!

Some of the Mexicans were so fired up that they tried to break into the hotel and one or two actually got up to our floor. Alf thought about taking us elsewhere, but then settled for sending the bus off as a decoy. It didn't work, and we simply had to suffer the malicious noise, with Alf growing more and more furious with the people who were supposed to be protecting us.

It was no sort of preparation for such an important match. England hadn't beaten Brazil since 1956 and, frustratingly, I never was to experience that pleasure. Neither was Bobby Moore, and we both played over a hundred games for our country.

We fancied ourselves this time. Brazil weren't better than us, although they always seem to have a hand grenade behind their backs. Just when you think you've got them, they yank out the pin, as they'd done in Rio the previous year, scoring twice after we'd led for most of the game.

When the news came that Gerson wouldn't be fit to take his place in midfield, our confidence soared. He was their organizer, an alert little man with marvellous vision, who struck the ball beautifully through the air with his left foot. He would be a great loss to them.

More so than Pele? I doubted it. Here was one of the greatest players of all time, perhaps the greatest, although my particular preference is for Alfredo di Stefano. Pele had looked thoroughly disillusioned in 1966 when Brazil fell apart, their morale undermined by poor selection and a crippling devotion to men who had begun to play from memory. Brazil went out before the quarter finals, and when Pele fell victim to the violent tackles launched at him by Morais of Portugal, he hinted that the World Cup had seen the last of him. But Pele's enthusiasm was apparently restored and we'd seen enough in Brazil's match against Czechoslovakia to feel that he was still supremely capable of winning a game on his own.

It was impossible to pigeonhole Pele. He was certainly a great goalscorer, the most prolific of all time. But he could also create, organize and inspire. Eyes set remarkably wide in a strong face accounted for the extraordinary extent of his vision. Only five feet seven inches tall, he gave the impression of being much larger when in the colours of his country or his club, Santos. Powerful muscles provided him with murderous pace and his imagination, allied to great natural gifts, never failed to thrill. Pele invented ways of playing the game. He could also head well and that talent was to provide Gordon Banks with an opportunity to impress his great skills on the competition.

Despite popular belief, Alf Ramsey didn't fill our heads with tactical detail. He merely emphasized that he had chosen us because we were, in his view, the best players in England. On this occasion he also stressed that careless passing would be even more destructive because of the energy required to regain the ball when playing at altitude and in smothering heat. We must try and keep our shape and not allow ourselves to become overstretched between defence and attack. We must work to ensure that there were enough players behind the ball whenever the Brazilians came at us.

We began well, stroking the ball around, feeling our way into the match, avoiding the errors that are always likely to occur in much tense circumstances. Then, after about ten minutes, we were suddenly turned by a lightning thrust along our left flank. Carlos Alberto fed Jairzinho who spurted past Terry Cooper to the byline. From there the winger's centre soared to the far post, some ten yards out. Pele had drifted behind Alan Mullery and now he came pounding in on Alan's blind side, thrusting upwards, body coiled.

Other players in the vicinity reported that in the very instant he smashed his head into the ball Pele had shouted, 'Goal!' Gordon Banks had a different opinion.

Having been drawn to the near post by Jairzinho's impressive run, he was hopelessly out of position when Pele fired in the header. But with a stupendous leap that was a product of hours spent going for our shots in practice, Gordon twisted backwards through the air, getting beneath the ball as it bounced up towards the net, then scooping it over the crossbar with his right hand.

A save that has been seen thousands of times since couldn't

fail to inspire us. I felt young again, my lungs were free, I was full of running and might have scored with a shot that rose, frustratingly, over the bar. I yearned for Wembley where the ball invariably keeps low.

It proved to be a marvellous match, not of the vibrant FA Cup tie kind, but a battle of wits, of thrust and counterthrust and brilliantly executed skills. A contest to enthrall anyone with a genuine feel for the greatest team game known to man.

After we'd seen it on film I was quoted like this: 'Even *we* were impressed. You could take the film and show it, confidently, to every young player in the world. It really is what the game at top level is all about. There is everything in it, all the skills and techniques, all the tactical control, the lot. There really was some special stuff played out there.' I have no reason to change my mind now.

Someone told us that Charlie Cooke shed a tear at the end. A Scot crying for England? No. Just one sensitive professional feeling for his own kind.

We should have won that match. We had the best chances, and after his stupendous save Gordon Banks didn't have much to do. Martin Peters had a marvellous opportunity to put us ahead, but there was an ingredient missing from his game in Mexico and he headed over. A brilliant footballer, Martin was at his most dangerous when stealing through with a footpad's cunning to find space for himself on the far post. In order to do that he had to cover a lot of ground and the conditions were against him.

A similar conclusion could be reached about Francis Lee, who was never the aggressively independent force we knew him to be back home. When Tommy Wright, benefiting from Alan Mullery's sensibly swift pass, sent the ball over, it looked as though Brazil's goal would fall. But Franny snatched at the chance and his thrusting, low header flew, agonizingly for us, straight at Felix.

Then came an opportunity for Bobby Moore to justify the bold assertion that he could cope with the most devilish of Brazil's free kicks. After being felled just outside the penalty area, Jairzinho infiltrated our wall as Brazil prepared to repeat the trick that had worked so well for them against the Czechs. But Bobby had indeed come up with the solution. He simply stood behind Jairzinho, and when Rivelino's shot tore through, our captain killed it as neatly as though he were dealing with a ball of cottonwool. The crowd gasped and I'm told that Alf actually smiled.

So it went on into the second half, the sun ferocious overhead, the heat draining the energy from our bodies. Then Brazil scored.

Tostao reminded me in many ways of Ian St. John whose play at centre forward was such a notable feature of Liverpool's surge to the forefront of British football. Short, sturdy and strong-legged, the Brazilian had no qualms about being isolated with his back to goal, hardly a predicament when his impressive physical and mental assets were taken into account. Tostao wasn't asked to make the extending runs that are still required of most British strikers. He was more of a darter, coming away from markers with a disconcerting swiftness, a manoeuvre that enabled him to exploit a talent for perfectly delivered first-time passes. Alternatively, he would collect the ball, turn and go for the throat! When he did this to Bobby Moore out on our left, we were in trouble. Having squirted the ball, somewhat luckily, through Bobby's legs, Tostao spun away from the men who were now bearing down on him and made enough room to get in a centre. It was a speculative effort, but our luck was out and the ball went to Pele, who slid it square. When Terry Cooper slipped there were no Englishmen left and Jairzinho pounced to drive the ball high into the net.

We didn't deserve to be behind, but Alf must have felt that drastic measures were necessary because, with some twenty minutes remaining, he sent out two substitutes, Colin Bell for me and Jeff Astle for Franny Lee. A considerable threat whenever the ball could be got to his head, Astle's availability on the touchline provided Alf with the option of going at

Brazil through the air and, with time running, out he took it up.

Ironically, Jeff's best chance came along the ground and he missed it, horribly, pulling a sloppy shot wide with his left foot. We held our heads, despair dissolving into sympathy for the big fella who, to be fair, might have made more of the opportunity had he been out there longer. On the other hand, I couldn't imagine that Brazil wouldn't have taken full advantage of such an opening.

Nevertheless, the wisdom of putting Jeff on was soon borne out when he got his head to Bobby Moore's centre, helping it on to where Alan Ball was free on the edge of the penalty area. There were no defenders within striking distance of Alan and as he shaped to shoot, I muttered 'Hit the target,' parroting what Jimmy Murphy used to preach so vehemently at Old Trafford. Alan didn't hit the target. Felix was completely beaten by the ball's flight but it hit the bar!

Nothing as clear-cut came our way again, but even though we ended up losing to Brazil, once more it had been a marvellous experience and the general feeling was that we could beat them if we met in the final.

I didn't feel unduly fatigued afterwards although when I looked in a mirror it was clear what this World Cup had begun to take out of me. The skin was drawn tight across my cheekbones and with very little camouflage on top I looked emaciated. We'd all lost an incredible amount of weight during the game – Alan Mullery was seven pounds lighter by the end – but the ingenious honeycombed tablets that enabled us to absorb adequate amounts of salt, releasing it slowly into our systems, had worked well. The lagers we were again allowed that night completed the recovery.

Later on in the year I was shown a photograph taken at Reading where I played for Manchester United about a month after returning from Mexico. I looked disturbingly thin.

It was now only necessary to avoid defeat against Czechoslovakia to be sure of a place in the quarter finals, and for a game in which I equalled Billy Wright's record of 105 England caps, Alf rested five men, including Geoff Hurst. This decision let in Allan Clarke of Leeds and we didn't have long to wait for an expression of the self-confidence that had helped to establish him as one of the deadliest finishers in the First Division.

Geoff's absence meant that someone would have to accept the responsibility for taking penalty kicks. Few players fancy the job and Alf was in no danger of being trampled underfoot when he called for volunteers. Then up went Allan's right arm. 'I'll take them,' he said casually, breaking the silence in our dressing room.

It was quite a burden Allan took on because although the odds were heavily in favour of us going through to the last eight with Brazil, the match was not without hazardous possibilities. If we lost by one goal, lots would have to be drawn to decide between us and Rumania. The Czechs needed to win by four goals, and a three-goal winning margin would send them into a lottery with the Rumanians for second place. As it turned out, the one goal that settled the match in our favour was a penalty given for handball four minutes into the second half. So Allan was put to the test in his very first game for England.

I'm told that when he swaggered forward to place the ball on the spot, a number of Englishmen could be heard expressing their concern, astonished that a newcomer to international football should be invested with such a severe challenge. They were instantly reassured by Billy Bremner, the Leeds captain.

'Sniffer is a hundred to one on,' forecast Billy confidently, using the name by which Clarke was known at Elland Road, one that arose from his talent for nosing out half chances. Billy's faith was fully justified. Allan lashed the ball unhesitatingly into the net.

That moment apart, it was an unsatisfactory affair and we were glad to get the last of our group games out of the way. As runners-up we were about to renew our long-standing rivalry with the West Germans, who had the advantage of remaining in León, where they had swept aside the opposition in Group 4 with an impressive goal difference of 10–4. León stands 1000 feet higher than Guadalajara, but altitude no longer frightened us and the general impression was that we were about to come onto a game.

When we arrived at our motel in León on the afternoon preceding the match, Mrs Franz Beckenbauer was with the wives of other German players by the swimming pool. Bobby Moore, Geoff Hurst, Martin Peters and Peter Bonetti also had their wives in Mexico, but that arrangement hadn't appealed to me. I would have been concerned for Norma's welfare in a strange country and we agreed that her presence was bound to be distracting. I certainly didn't want to be exposed to the suggestion that my mind wasn't entirely on the World Cup, particularly as some reporters had been sent out specifically to monitor our behaviour off the field.

In that respect I was aware of a disturbing new trend that would continue to gather momentum. Television was taking the World Cup live into millions of homes around the globe and because of the vast interest newspapers were no longer content merely to cover the matches and the news they generated. Some of them were constantly on the lookout for scandal, and a chance remark made in a bar or even the hotel lobby might explode into tomorrow's headline.

I make those points partly out of sympathy for Peter Bonetti, who was to suffer the malicious suggestion that he wasn't in the right frame of mind to deputise when Gordon Banks fell ill in León.

The source of the sickness remains a mystery, the most plausible explanation being that he'd foolishly disregarded the warnings we'd had about iced drinks, although both Keith Newton and I had experienced some slight discomfort. It was to be suggested that Gordon was the victim of a CIA plot designed to keep the Brazilians happy, but I found that too daft to warrant serious consideration.

No one was more devastated by Gordon's condition than

Neil Phillips, the team doctor who had mothered us for six weeks in Latin America, not only tending to our aches and pains but ensuring that our systems weren't violated. That it should be Gordon who went down at such a critical time was atrocious luck for the Doc.

We knew something was wrong when Gordon failed to turn out for a light training session, but he had a reasonable night and was able to do ball work on the morning of the match. We were relieved when he showed up for the team meeting prior to our departure for the stadium which, in fact, was only a few hundred yards from the motel. It seemed then as though the crisis had passed, but as the meeting progressed Gordon began to feel unwell again and was put to bed. It was then that Peter Bonetti learned that he was about to play in a World Cup for the first time. I glanced across at him, wondering how he felt. Barely an hour to go and the responsibility enormous. He also must have sensed our apprehension. Gordon was more than just a great goalkeeper in our eyes. As I have said, he was probably the most important player in the competition and now we were going out to face the Germans without the reassuring sight of him in goal.

England were well off for keepers and I'm sure that Peter and Alex Stepney would have walked into most of the other teams. But Banks was Banks. Exceptional, unique. With no disrespect to Peter, we wouldn't have lost to the Germans if Gordon had played. Gordon to my knowledge had never let in three when playing for England. But that's getting ahead of the game.

We murmured our good wishes to Peter in the dressing room beforehand and then strode out into the sun. A strange place, León, a pleasant enough city but not one that had responded completely to the World Cup. A group of Britons had arrived there to discover that their hotel rooms were already occupied and spent hours trying to arrange alternative accommodation. They were eventually fixed up in a monastery! And so it was in the early hours of the morning that the monks were woken by a well-lubricated rendering of

119

'It's a grand old team to play for' as a rare old team straggled in from a night on the town.

It was to a blast of klaxons that we took the field against the Germans who, as always, were going to use tight man-to-man marking backed up by a free 'sweep' defender. They wouldn't alter that system although it never seemed to work that well against us because of the amount of running we were willing to do. Geoff Hurst, who applied himself so intelligently to the task of taking defenders into places where they were instantly uncomfortable was always a problem for German opposition and I instinctively knew right from the off that this would be one of his great matches. Geoff was playing so well in advanced positions that we soon possessed the confidence to get forward and support him.

As in the final at Wembley four years earlier, the Germans had detailed Beckenbauer to mark me, and even though I was by then thirty-four years old, Franz didn't seem to fancy the task. I felt marvellous, the best I'd felt since the World Cup began. My legs were strong and it was as though I'd got energy to burn. I felt even better when Alan Mullery put us ahead with a memorable shot. Alan began the move with a searching cross-field pass to Keith Newton, who strode forward on his long legs. In the meantime, Alan himself had set off upfield, taking a diagonal line through the German defenders who, amazingly, made no attempt to cut him off. When Keith's centre came in, Alan arrived with perfect timing to sweep the ball past Sepp Maier.

The second half had barely got under way when we scored again. Keith Newton and Terry Cooper had unnerved the Germans with their runs along the flanks, and Keith contributed marvellously again, sprinting onto Geoff Hurst's pass to send it beyond the far post where Martin Peters resurrected his gift for showing up when least expected. He forced the ball past Maier and we had every reason to believe that we were on our way. It was then that Germany brought on Grabowski.

Grabowski was the original 'Supersub', coming on late to

run the legs off wearied defenders. Helmut Schoen, the German manager, sent for Grabowski like a general pitching in a crack cavalry squadron to try to save a battle. But there were only twenty minutes left and our defence was reckoned to be the best in Mexico.

It was Beckenbauer who scored. He'd tried a shot that Franny Lee blocked and the ball rebounded luckily to his feet. As Franz went at Alan Mullery, I could hear Alf's instruction in the team talk. 'If Beckenbauer gets to our box, don't let him work the ball onto his right foot.' But it was to the right that Alan let him go, though Franz was so wide of the target he didn't seem to present too great a threat. Not until Peter Bonetti so mistimed his plunge at a half-hit shot that he was unable to prevent the ball reaching our net. It was a terrible experience for the Chelsea man, who must have known what we were all saying to ourselves. It was quite simply that Gordon would have kept the shot out. I didn't know it, but the curtain was about to fall upon my international career. Looking ahead to the next match, Alf had already decided to send out Colin Bell in my place, and he did so now, within a minute of Beckenbauer's goal. I wasn't happy about that, but Alf had brought me off before and I was the oldest in the team. He apologized on the plane home after asking me to sit with him for a while.

Successful substitutions are rarely the triumphs they often appear to be. A manager invariably changes his team out of desperation, hoping that a fresh face will turn the tide. Alf had something more definite in mind and how close he came to recovering the initiative.

Colin Bell broke instantly along the right, and when Geoff Hurst dived in low to meet the centre, the ball flew from his head to the far post. It looked certain to go in or at worst to come back off the upright to where Franny Lee was following up. If Franny had carried on he could have tapped in a goal. Instead he stood (as he was to admit) mesmerized and the ball rolled harmlessly over the byline. If another substitution had to be made at this stage, I would have sent on someone for Terry Cooper who was struggling to cope with Grabowski. It was Norman Hunter who went on and almost immediately the Germans scored again. Brian Labone ought to have cleared from our penalty area but only succeeded in sending the ball to Schnellinger who fed it back to Uwe Seeler on the far side of goal. That sturdy little man propelled himself upwards, getting in a back header that carried no definite aim. But Peter Bonetti had got himself caught in no-man's-land and the ball dropped over him and under the bar.

At that stage my brother Jack left his seat in the stand and went out into the street. His club, Leeds United, were a superstitious lot. They'd been pipped for both the League championship and the FA Cup the previous season and Jack admitted to me that when the Germans equalized after Norman Hunter came on he was convinced that nothing good could happen to anyone from Leeds that year. Jack was still wandering about outside when the West Germans beat us in extra time with Muller's acrobatic overhead volley.

It was agony sitting through those twenty minutes when we gave it all away, but I don't recall much about the immediate aftermath. Most of us had been at it too long for tears and I can remember Alan Mullery repeating over and over again, 'We were bloody fireproof. We were going all the way.'

Back at the motel we discovered that Gordon Banks, watching a delayed TV transmission in his room, still thought we were leading 2–0 until Alex Stepney came in to break the news.

We changed into swimming trunks and gathered around the pool and I broke out the wine I'd ordered to celebrate my record collection of 106 caps.

Alf stayed in his chalet for a long time and a visitor was to find him slumped in a chair, sipping champagne and murmuring to no one in particular about the massive misfortune that had cost us Gordon Banks.

'Of all the players to lose, we had to lose him,' Alf said, repeating the words over and over again.

He emerged to join us and a party developed as the night

drew on. We drank some and sang some. I'd had marvellous times in the England team. I'd been a part of four World Cups beginning in 1958 when, although not getting a game, I'd travelled to Sweden. I'd played with and against great players and I wanted to continue.

We would have beaten Italy in the semifinals, no doubt about that, and I don't think Brazil would have fancied playing us in the final. They were as superstitious as Our Kid's lot. They'd struggled to beat us in Rio the previous summer and again in Guadalajara. Maybe it would have been our turn. Maybe.

Career Record

Honours
World Cup Winners Medal 1966
European Cup Winners Medal 1968
League Championship Medals 1957, 1965, 1967
FA Cup Winners Medal 1963
FA Cup Runners-up Medals 1957, 1958
European Footballer of the Year 1966
Footballer of the Year 1966

Appearances (Manchester United)	League		International	
	Games	Goals	Games	Goals
1956–57	14	10		
1957–58	21	8	3	3
1958–59	38	29	9	8
1959–60	37	13	6	2
1960–61	39	21	9	8
1961–62	37	8	12	4
1962–63	28	7	6	5
1963–64	40	9	10	3
1964–65	41	10	3	1
1965–66	38	16	16	6
1966–67	42	12	4	1
1967–68	41	15	9	5
1968–69	32	5	8	1
1969–70	40	12	11	2
1970–71	42	5		
1971–72	40	8		
1972–73	34	6		
	606	**198**	**106**	**49**
(Preston North End)				
1973–74	**38**	**8**		